Java and Internet Security

Java™ and Internet Security

Theodore J. Shrader,

Bruce A. Rich,

Anthony J. Nadalin

iUniverse.com, Inc.

San Jose   New York   Lincoln   Shanghai

Java and Internet Security

Published by iUniverse.com, Inc.

For information address:
iUniverse.com, Inc.
620 North 48th Street, Suite 201
Lincoln, NE 68504-3467
www.iuniverse.com

ISBN: 0-595-13500-5

Printed in the United States of America

To my wonderful wife Mary and son Benjamin who bring joy to my life.

To my partner in life and love, Gail, and her watch care over our four children while I focus on this book.

To Paula, queen of joy, and Sarah, the princess of fun, who keep me focused on reality.

Contents

List of Illustrations

Foreword

I am delighted to read this new book on Java security and its application in the context of Internet security, written by some of the industry's best practitioners on the subject.

Java security by now is no longer a novel subject known only to people on the cutting edge of Internet technologies. Along with the wide adoption of Java technology in the computer industry, Java security has become a mainstream technology that is being used everyday in many industry sectors and government agencies. Java security is a cornerstone of some of these applications, especially for the financial industry.

Since the basic Java security model debuted with Java technology in 1995, fundamental improvements have been made to the design and implementation of Java security technology, most notably with the introduction of policy-driven, fine-grained, flexible, and extensible access control as part of the Java 2 Standard Edition (formerly known as JDK 1.2—Java Development Kit 1.2) that was officially released in December of 1998.

Vertically, the Java platform provides a comprehensive set of intrinsic security features. For example, the Java language is strongly typed to provide a better and safer programming environment, and type safety is checked both at code-load time and during runtime. Moreover, access to crucial system resources such as the file system is mediated by the Java Virtual Machine. A security policy dictates who can access which resources in what manner. (For grueling details of subtle design rationales, please refer to my book entitled "Inside Java 2 Platform Security" published by Addison-Wesley in June of 1999.)

Horizontally, the Java platform additionally provides a whole range of building blocks that are fundamental to any system that requires end-to-end security. For example, the Java Cryptography Architecture (implemented in JDK 1.2 and in the Java Cryptography Extension 1.2) provides primitives for encryption and digital signature technologies, including crypto key generation and management, crypto algorithms (such as DES and Triple-DES, DSA and RSA, SHA-1 and MD5), and other convenience tools. The Java Secure Socket Extension 1.0 enables secure Internet communications, such as secure passage of data between a client and a server running HTTP, by implementing SSL (Secure Sockets Layer) and TLS (Transport Layer Security) protocols with functionality for message integrity, data encryption, server authentication, and client authentication. In addition, the Java Authentication and Authorization Service 1.0 can be used to determine who is currently executing

Java code and supplement the code-based security framework provided by JDK 1.2 with user-based access control.

As Sun's Chief Java Security Architect from 1996 to 1999, it has been exciting to direct these projects and to watch them come to fruition. Our colleagues at IBM have been intimately involved with the development of these Java security technology standards and thus are in an excellent position to write such a well-organized and easy-to-read guide book for Java security programmers. The book covers both the vertical and horizontal aspects of Java security and provides many working examples. I am confident that you will enjoy the book.

In the past two years, Java technology has expanded to include Java 2 Enterprise Edition and Java 2 Micro Edition. Not surprisingly, Java security technology is following that expansion. For example, the most requested new feature for the recent version of Personal Java 3.1 is JDK 1.2 style security. The just-released Service Gateway specification 1.0 (by the Open Service Gateway Initiative – an industry group consisting of more than 60 major international companies defining an open standard for connecting and provisioning services to the new generation of smart consumer and business appliances – where I served as its founding Java Expert Group Chair) also depends on JDK 1.2 style security features for fine-grained access control. Very soon similar security features will be integrated into Java standards for enterprise and e-commerce applications as well as for smart-cards, cellular phones, TVs and set-top boxes, and other household appliances. As the saying goes, you ain't seen nothing yet.

Li Gong, Ph.D.
Director, Server Products
Consumer and Embedded Division
Sun Microsystems, Inc.
Cupertino, California
July 2000

Acknowledgements

We would like to thank the many folks who helped make this book possible. Suzette Minorini, our IBM Java Security team manager, has given us her enthusiastic support and encouragement along the way. Karen Foley, Jean Swanson, and Mike Rainer of the IBM DeveloperToolbox team have also been generous in their support of this endeavor. Jean provided us with valuable comments, and Mike helped create the illustrations in this book. Our appreciation goes to Herb Hintz for his thoughts and suggestions as well.

Thanks also to Li Gong, Director of the Server Products Group and a Distinguished Engineer with Sun Microsystems, Inc., and Hemma Prafullchandra, the Director of Security Engineering & Research with Critical Path Inc. and a previous member of the original Sun Java Security team, for giving us invaluable technical feedback. We thank Maxine Erlund, Jan Luhe, Charlie Lai, Sharon Liu, and all the members of the Sun Java Security team for their time, dedication, and talent. (Our thoughts and prayers go with Charlie on his road back to good health.)

Lastly, we would like to thank the other members of the IBM Java Security team who helped us bring this important technology to the marketplace: Larry Koved, Joyce Leung, Marco Pistoia, Kent Soper, Audrey Timkovich, Krishna Yellepeddy, and Yanni Zhang.

List of Abbreviations

AES	Advanced Encryption Standard
API	Application Programming Interface
CA	Certificate Authority
CMP	Certificate Management Protocol
CRL	Certificate Revocation List
CSP	Cryptographic Service Provider
DCE	Distributed Computing Environment
DER	Distinguished Encoding Rules
DES	Data Encryption Standard
DSA	Digital Signature Algorithm
EE	End Entity
GSSAPI	Generic Security Service Application Program Interface
HTML	Hypertext Markup Language
HTTP	Hypertext Transfer Protocol
HTTPS	Secure Hypertext Transfer Protocol
IBMJCE	IBM Java Cryptography Extension
IETF	Internet Engineering Task Force
J2SE	Java 2 Standard Edition
JAAS	Java Authentication and Authorization Services
JCA	Java Cryptography Architecture
JCE	Java Cryptography Extension

JDK	Java Development Kit
JKS	Java KeyStore
JRE	Java Runtime Environment
JSSE	Java Secure Sockets Extension
JVM	Java Virtual Machine
KDC	Key Distribution Center
LDAP	Lightweight Directory Access Protocol
MAC	Message Authentication Code
MIME	Multipurpose Internet Mail Extensions
MIT	Massachusetts Institute of Technology
NIST	National Institute of Standards and Technology
PKCS	Public Key Cryptography Standards
PKI	Public Key Infrastructure
PKIX	Public Key Infrastructure X.509
RA	Registration Authority
RSA	RSA public-key cryptosystem
SDK	Standard Development Kit
S/MIME	Secure/Multipurpose Internet Mail Extensions
SSL	Secure Sockets Layer
TLS	Transport Layer Security
URL	Uniform Resource Locator

Trademarks

IBM, DB2, WebSphere, MQSeries, and SecureWay are trademarks or registered trademarks of IBM in the U.S. and other countries.

Sun, Solaris, Java™ and all Java-based trademarks are trademarks or registered trademarks of Sun Microsystems, Inc. in the U.S. and other countries.

Netscape is a registered trademark of Netscape Communications Corporation in the United States and other countries.

Microsoft, Windows, Windows NT, Windows 2000 are either registered trademarks or trademarks of Microsoft Corporation in the United States and/or other countries.

Other product and service names may be trademarks or service marks of their respective owners.

Introduction

Welcome to your guidebook to the realm of Java and Internet security. Within these pages, we'll introduce you to the hottest security topics for building and understanding successful e-business applications. Our tour begins with an introduction to the Java 2 security model and its objects. Next, we dive into cryptography and explain the latest cryptographic extensions. No security book would be complete without a thorough explanation of the public key technologies, their role with digital signatures and on the Internet, and the imperative to use them in e-business. We wrap up our discussion with a smorgasbord of security topics, including the Java Secure Sockets Extension (JSSE), Java Authentication and Authorization Services (JAAS), and lastly, Kerberos.

Whether you are new to security or a guru, we offer introductory and advanced discussions of the latest security technologies. We've designed our book into several complimentary sections for easy reading. Each section contains a number of articles that can be read individually for a quick overview or as a whole to gain an in-depth discussion of the topic. We've included selected articles from the IBM DeveloperToolbox (formally known as the IBM Developer Connection) magazine with revisions for the latest release of the Java platform. We've also included new articles and a generous helping of code samples.

As a software engineer, architect, IT specialist, or someone who is interested in the latest technologies in the security realm, we welcome you to the exciting world of Java and Internet security.

Introduction to Java Security

In this section, we introduce you to the Java 2 security model and provide detail on its many objects and abilities.

- Scouting Java security

- Foray into Java security objects

- Protection domains and checking permissions in Java security

- Applets and Java security

- Implementing custom security permissions in Java security

Scouting Java security

When the Java technology first burst upon the programming scene, it appealed to programmers for many reasons. Some were drawn to the Java environment because of its ease of programming, some because of its robustness and memory management, some because of its cross-platform capabilities, some because of its built-in language and runtime security, and others possibly even because of its appealing name and the marketing glitz surrounding it.

In part because of the broad nature of the Java platform's appeal, this wide spectrum of programmers may interpret *security* in many different, possibly conflicting ways. This article will discuss why the Java language is said to be secure, and discuss the evolution of the Java technologies to incorporate more and more security features.

Java Language Security

The Java language itself has some key features that lend themselves to development of more secure programs. The first feature of Java security that we will focus on here is its enforcement of access policies. Every method, object and primitive data element in a Java program has one of the following access levels associated with it:

- Private

  Can only be accessed by code that is contained in the class that defines the method, object, or primitive.

- Unspecified (This is the default, also known as package access)

  Can be accessed by any class that is in the same package as the class defining the method, object, or primitive.

- Protected

  Can be accessed by any class that is in the same package as the class defining the method, object, or primitive, or by any class that subclasses the defining class.

- Public

  Can be accessed by code in any class and any package.

With the exception of package, these access levels correspond to keywords in the Java language. Although specification of access levels similar to these is shared with many other object-oriented languages, the Java language enforces them to an extent rarely seen elsewhere. The point of all this is to maintain strict control over access to data or objects in memory. The Java architecture dictates that:

- Access levels are strictly enforced during runtime.

  In the Java architecture, a private entity will always be treated as private. This provides a rare degree of comfort to the original programmer, as other programs or programmers cannot undo a careful design.

- Programs are prohibited from accessing unauthorized memory locations.

  The Java architecture does not even have the notion of a pointer. This helps minimize all kinds of useful (usually in a very shortsighted, later-regretted way) optimizations, as well as a wide variety of errors and security or integrity holes.

- Object typing is strictly enforced.

  One cannot simply cast between an int and an Object, for example. This precludes programmatic data corruption. One may only cast an object to either one of its superclasses or one of its subclasses (if indeed the object is an instance of that subclass).

- Final primitives, objects, methods, and classes cannot be changed at runtime.

  In the Java architecture, constants are declared with the final qualifier. If the platform were to allow modifications of a constant, a program's behavior could be controlled from outside. The Java language precludes this. Methods may be declared as final too, preventing subclasses from overriding them. Classes may be declared as final also, which helps prevent the adding of new behaviors through subclassing.

- Operations on uninitialized variables are not allowed.

  This keeps Java programs from being able to snoop the contents of virtual memory left from the previous user of that memory.

- Array bounds are checked on all array accesses.

  The prime benefit here is in terms of more robust programs, but the failure to do this can result in memory overwrites, which could be exploited to breach security and/or corrupt data.

Turning Homily into Reality

The rules above are fine as general programming practice, but mean little if they are not enforced. The Java architecture automatically enforces these rules. This enforcement may happen at three distinct times in the lifecycle of a Java program: at compile time, when a class is loaded into the virtual machine, and at runtime. Not all rules can be checked at each point, but whatever can be done will be done at each point to help ensure the protection of entities in memory. Please keep in mind that the final arbiter of a Java program's correctness will be the virtual machine, and that will be the place where runtime checks, like those of array bounds or object casting, will take place. Note also that any calls out of Java code into native code (where these rules are not enforced) risks the integrity of all that has gone on before. For maximum return on your security investment, stay in Java code. Does that mean it is impossible to write bad Java code? Obviously not, but it is easier for an average developer to write good Java code, and harder to write bad code.

The Evolution of Java Security

Now that we understand some of the ways the Java language itself is secure, we must turn our attention to the way the Java architecture lets various programs interact with the host machine and its resources. This is called the Java Security Model.

The Original Sandbox Model

The original security model provided by the Java platform is known as the sandbox model. (The Java platform is code written in the Java language, plus the support received from the attendant tools, classes and virtual machine.) The sandbox model found in the Java Development Kit (JDK) 1.0 from Sun separates the world into the haves and the have-nots. The haves are any classes found on the CLASSPATH. These classes are assumed to have all privileges and powers available to them, and are not even subject to class verification upon load, although all Java code runs under the watchful eye of the Java Virtual Machine (JVM). The have-nots are classes loaded via a ClassLoader, and would thus include downloaded remote code such as applets. These have-nots are untrusted, and can access only the limited resources available inside the sandbox. In particular, they cannot get to the local file system, and can only interact with other classes loaded by the same ClassLoader. This sandbox model is illustrated in **Figure 1**.

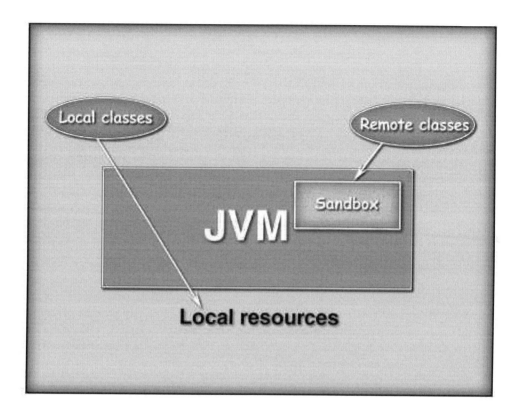

Figure 1: Java 1.0 security model

The Modified Sandbox Model

JDK 1.1 from Sun modified the Sandbox Model slightly, allowing digitally signed applets out of the sandbox. Signed applets in 1.1 are treated as trusted local code, if the signature key is recognized as trusted by the end system that receives the applet. These signed applets, along with their signatures, are delivered in the Java Archive format (JAR). If, however, the signature is unrecognized, or the applet is unsigned, it runs in the sandbox. This model is illustrated in **Figure 2**.

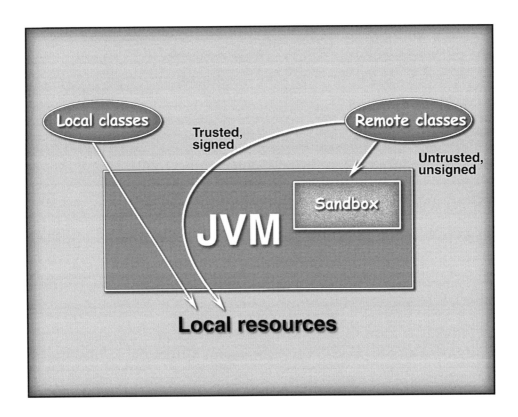

Figure 2: Java 1.1 security model

The Java 2 Security Architecture

In Java 2 security, many things changed. A partial list follows:

•   Fine-grained access control.

One no longer has to adopt a binary trust model where one either trusts a class or not, but instead one can apply a much lower granularity of trust to a class or collection of classes. For example, a user or administrator can specify that a particular class or collection of classes has permission to read a file or files from a file system, but does not have permission to write anything there. The previous levels of the Java platform could only be directed to either completely trust the class, or not trust it with anything outside the sandbox.

- Extension of security checks to all Java programs, including applications as well as applets.

  Java 2 security allows local code to be subjected to the same security controls as applets, although it is possible to configure the security policy to allow some or all local code to run as totally trusted, if desired.

- Easily configurable security policy.

  The security policy is externalized in a file (specified via Uniform Resource Locator (URL), so it may be either local or remote), which can be easily extended by programmers, tailored by administrators, and tweaked by individual users, as desired.

This model is illustrated in **Figure 3**

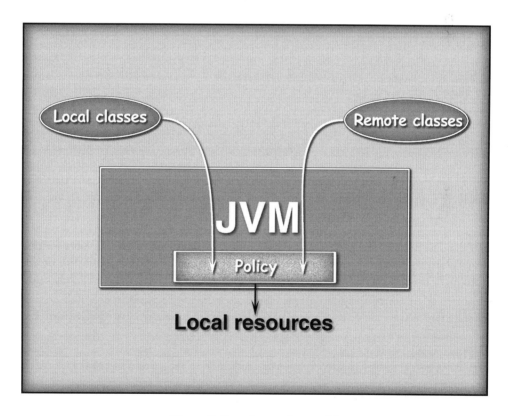

Figure 3: Java 2 security model

Functional Evolution

Let's recap what we've covered so far. We've discussed the Java language security, as well as the evolution of its security model. Well, more than the security model has been changing! In part due to the Java platform's rapid acceptance in the programming world, many new requirements have been levied against it in the area of security, and the Java architecture has risen to the challenge. Each new release has added features that contribute to the security of the Java platform. A very abbreviated list of the new security features follows:

- Authentication

  In Java 1.1 security, the author (or more commonly, the author's company) could sign classes so that one could know the origins of the class, and either extend trust on that basis, or not.

- Policy-driven

  Java 2 security provides an extensible, configurable security policy to drive the security engine.

- Cryptography

  Java 1.1 security introduced the Java Cryptography Architecture (JCA), as well as a Java Cryptography Extension (JCE), to allow pluggable cryptography for the construction of secure applications. Java 2 security further improves on the JCA and JCE.

- Auditing

  This is possible on any level of the Java platform, if one provides one's own auditing SecurityManager.

We expect that continuing acceptance of Java technologies will drive more and more security content into the Java platform. But do not overlook the significance of the Java platform's contributions to date. The Java platform has the ability to protect the information on a computer from being accessed or modified, while still allowing the Java program to run on that computer, no matter what its operating system or hardware. This strength has been and continues to be a strong reason for its rapid deployment and acceptance.

Foray into Java 2 security objects

In this article, we provide an overview to the Java security objects and files used in the Java 2 platform. This article also provides an example of a Java program that runs with a Java security policy.

Unless specifically mentioned, whenever this article mentions the use of an object or execution of an operation in a Java program, Java applications and applets are included. If Java applets deviate from the behavior of Java programs, the text will call out their differences.

Important players

The following classes play important roles in the Java 2 security model. Other classes, such as certificates and class loaders, also play a role, but the classes described below are the most frequent ones that Java programs are cognizant of or use:

- Permission
- PermissionCollection
- CodeSource
- ProtectionDomain
- Policy
- AccessController
- AccessControlContext

Permission class

The Permission class represents what the program can do, such as read a file or access a system property. The class itself is abstract, so one must subclass the Permission class to provide an actual implementation. Permissions that do not require a parameter other than the name of the permission itself, such as access to a package or being able to exit the Java Virtual Machine (JVM), typically subclass the BasicPermission class. Other permissions that require parameters to be associated with the name, such as the exact operations permitted on a file of a particular name, typically subclass the Permission class.

The Java Runtime Environment (JRE) itself uses a number of system-defined permissions that extend the Permission class and its subclasses.

User-defined permission classes can subclass any of the Permission class tree, but they must supply implementations for each of the abstract methods in the Permission class, as well as implement both the Serializable and Guard interfaces. The real power in the Permission class comes from the implies() method, which each implementer must supply. By requiring both an equals() and an implies() method, but implementing access control via the implies() method, Java 2 security allows for a more flexible and usable grammar for expressing access control. The equals() method tests for strict equality, and a permission class might implement implies() by simply calling equals(), but the real intent of implies() was to allow for subset tests. For example, a FilePermission allows subtree permission, so a request to access "file:/c:/a/b/c" is implied in a permission granted for "file:/c:/a/-" (the subtree mounted at c:/a) or "file:/c:/a/b/*" (all files in the directory c:/a/b).

Java 2 security also allows permissions to be grouped in a PermissionCollection (groups of permissions of identical types) or Permissions (groups of heterogeneous PermissionCollections) object. These classes support the implies() method, so checking for access, whether one has a single permission to check or a whole set of things to examine, starts off with a single call.

CodeSource class

The CodeSource class brings together a URL (codebase) with zero or more certificates (signers). A CodeSource need not have any certificates, indicating that classes loaded from the URL are unsigned. A URL may either point to the local file system or a remote server. Local and remote programs operate under the permissions granted for the codebases in the policy file. Only system classes run in a system domain where they can operate with impunity. This model differs from pre-Java 2 security where local programs operated with looser restrictions than remote programs.

ProtectionDomain class

The ProtectionDomain class relates a CodeSource object to a set of Permissions. The JVM uses a class loader to load a class from a particular URL. By virtue of the URL from which it was loaded, each class will operate with the set of Permissions associated with the class' CodeSource in the CodeSource's ProtectionDomain. Given that a specific class can only be loaded from one CodeSource, the class can only belong to one ProtectionDomain.

When an executing program tries to access a protected resource, the JVM will consult the ProtectionDomain objects related to all the classes on the execution stack frame. If the required Permission exists in the PermissionCollection for each ProtectionDomain object, the action is allowed. For example, if class A is loaded from one CodeSource and calls class B from another CodeSource, the Permissions for the ProtectionDomain objects associated with class A and B would be consulted. The required Permission would need to exist in both ProtectionDomain objects.

There is a way to bypass checking all the ProtectionDomain objects on the execution stack frames. If the JVM detects a doPrivilege code block within a method, the JVM will not check the ProtectionDomain objects on the stack prior to the current one. The skipped ProtectionDomain objects belong to the caller of the method containing the doPrivilege. Continuing with the same example, if the method in class B on the stack implements a doPrivilege block, only the ProtectionDomain for the CodeSource for class B would be consulted, not class A's ProtectionDomain. Note that class B still needs permission to perform the action, even though the caller, class A, does not.

Policy class

The abstract Policy class is implemented by the PolicyFile class, which embodies the Java policy file that contains a set of Permissions for a set of CodeSource objects. The PolicyFile class provides the default mechanism for reading a policy definition from a file. Java 2 security supplies a default flat ASCII policy file, but that need not be the only format. By specifying a different implementation in the Java security file, a program could override the behavior of the Policy object to instead have policy defined by a database, PKCS #12 file, or other resources besides than the default policy file. Though many may be defined, only one policy can be in effect at a time depending on what class the program has loaded.

AccessController class

In Java 2 security, the SecurityManager has evolved into the AccessController. It is no longer an abstract class, as with Java 1.1 security. Java 2 security still uses the SecurityManager, but recommends that future programs use the AccessController class as their gateway to controlling or consulting access to system resources. One of the most common ways for programs to use the AccessController class is to call the class' checkPermission method to see if the Permission object passed in as a parameter has been granted to the program. If the Permission was not granted by the policy, the method throws an AccessControlException.

Additionally, programs can use the AccessController to establish a privileged block within the code. The privileged block temporarily supplants the normal process for permission checking. The previous ProtectionDomain class section in this article described how the AccessController.doPrivileged() block affects the matching of permissions.

AccessControlContext class

A related class to the AccessController, AccessControlContext acts like a looking glass into the Java program's current calling context. Programs can retrieve the current AccessControlContext by calling the AccessController getContext() method. The AccessControlContext object captures the state of an AccessController and allows the stored state to be passed to other methods that may need to reference a state that's different from the current one. For example, this ability allows the program to pass a context from one thread to another thread that might be in charge of checking the permissions on a remembered context. In this scenario, the second thread can call the checkPermission method on the AccessControlContext object.

Security and policy files

Two files play an important role in the Java 2 security model. A JVM will have one Java security file that defines the basic building blocks of security, such as where to read the Java policy files from and what class represents the policy object. With the default representation provided in Java 2 security, users or administrators can grant policy through one or more policy files. Policy files are additive and each Java policy file can contain one or more sets of permissions associated with different codebases. Additionally, permissions in a policy file can be associated with a KeyStore, which contain certificates and possibly, their private keys. The default proprietary Java keystore type is "JKS," and administrators can use the supplied keytool program to create and manage JKS keystores.

Classes that do not match the codebase or signers in the policy file are placed in a default *sandbox* with a default set of permissions. For Windows NT version 3.5.1 or later, the default Java system security and policy files are located in $(java.home)\lib\security\java.security and $(java.home)\lib\security\java.policy. The default user policy file is located in $(user.home)\.java.policy. The default set of permissions for the *sandbox* is defined in the policy file and can be changed by the user or administrator.

During runtime, the policy object will combine Permissions as appropriate. For example, if a set of permissions is associated with certificate alias X and another set is associated with certificate alias Y and URL A, a class loaded from URL A and signed with certificates X and Y will have a set of permissions resulting from the combination of both sets.

Users can define the system and user policy files in effect for a Java program. However, the architecture of the Java 2 security model allows an administrator to define a single uniform policy via policy files throughout the enterprise environment, and thus prevent users, who may not be knowledgeable of the format or meaning of the Java policy file, from needing to know about the security model.

Security example

The following is a sample Java program that tries to read the contents of the local Windows NT file c:\antietam.txt. If user Benjamin tries to run the program with his default system and user java.policy file, he will discover that it lacks the proper permissions to perform this action.

FileReadExample.java

```
package ibm.book;

import java.io.*;
import java.security.*;

public class FileReadExample {

    public static void main(String argv[]) {
        String filename = "c:\\antietam.txt";
        String line = null;

        try {
            System.out.println("Trying to read from file " + filename + ".\n");

            BufferedReader infile =
                new BufferedReader(new FileReader(filename));
            while ((line = infile.readLine()) != null) {
                System.out.println(line);
            }
        }
```

```
   catch (AccessControlException e) {
       System.out.println("** Exception:  Need FilePermission read for " +
           filename + ".");
   }
   catch (Exception e) {
       System.out.println("** Exception:  " + e.toString());
       e.printStackTrace();
   }


   }
}
```

Since the program lacks the appropriate permission for the operation, the file read operation will throw an AccessControlException. The program will catch the exception and print out the FilePermission required error message.

By adding the following permission entry to Ben's user java.policy file, the program will succeed:

```
   permission java.io.FilePermission "c:\\antietam.txt", "read";
```

Conclusion

Java 2 security provides more granular security control to users and allows administrators to apply a consistent policy of permissions across the enterprise environment. A plethora of classes take part in security, but each builds upon the others and in turn, invites the others to the policy dance.

Protection domains and checking permission in Java security

With the Java 2 platform, Sun took an evolutionary step in its security architecture. Previous versions of Java security confined some code, such as applets, to a local sandbox. The code also did not automatically have permission to perform sensitive operations, such as reading and writing to the local drive. Java security considered other code trusted, like classes on the CLASSPATH, and allowed trusted code to run freely without hindrances.

Java 2 security unifies the security model by forcing all code outside of the Java core classes to go through a policy that grants permissions according to user or administrator preferences. Java 2 security also introduces several new packages and objects. This article explores the intricacies of the ProtectionDomain object, one of the premiere objects in the new Java 2 security model, and dives into an example of permission checking in this new world.

Protection domains

ProtectionDomain objects play key roles in the Java security arena. A ProtectionDomain object brings together other objects and collections whose relationships are essential for establishing authorization. **Figure 4** shows one possible instantiation of a ProtectionDomain and the objects that it contains. A glance at the ProtectionDomain object in this figure shows that it holds a CodeSource and a Permissions object. The CodeSource object wrappers a URL object and Certificate array. The Permissions object collects two PermissionCollection objects, each holding a different set of homogenous Permission objects. Before examining the ProtectionDomain class, it's important to understand the role of the objects that comprise the ProtectionDomain and build the way to the ProtectionDomain itself.

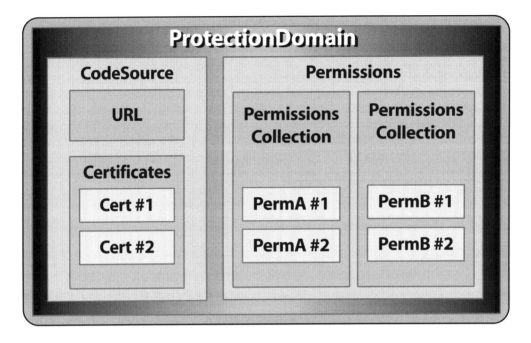

Figure 4: Sample ProtectionDomain object

Two questions about security infrastructure that need to be answered are: Where did the class come from and who created it? Identity is a fundamental aspect in security, and location is used to implement identity. The URL class with its attributes of protocol, host, port, and file reveals from where a class was loaded. For example, a class can have a protocol of HTTP or file, depending on whether the class was loaded remotely or locally. Developers also can sign their classes before distribution and that's where the Certificate class enters the fray. The Certificate class represents the signing identity of who created the class.

CodeSource

The CodeSource object fuses the location and signing attributes of a class together by combining a URL and array of Certificate objects. A class can be signed with one or more certificates, or with none at all. Every class can trace its lineage back to a single CodeSource object.

The CodeSource object forms one side of the equation, but a ProtectionDomain wouldn't be complete without permissions. The two objects together tell Java security what permissions have been granted for classes loaded from the related CodeSource. The Permission class and its subclasses act as fundamental wrappers or guards around resources. Other classes in Java security help ensure protection by checking if a permission has been granted for a class or stack of classes before allowing the action to be performed. For example, before the System.getProperty method can succeed, the corresponding PropertyPermission must be granted.

Permissions must be explicitly granted or Java 2 security assumes they are denied. Java 2 security doesn't have the concept of an explicit negative permission. As a default backing store, Java security supports an ASCII policy file that groups together a set of granted permissions for a URL, a signer, or both. Permissions can also be granted to all CodeSource objects. If a permission isn't part of the configured policy files, it isn't granted.

Java security provides a variety of predefined permission classes or developers can create their own. For example, PropertyPermission and RuntimePermission are basic permission classes referenced by Java methods in the Java core classes. Other permissions subclass the Permission class, such as SocketPermission or a user defined permission. Many permissions require only one parameter, signifying access to the resource, but other permissions take parameters. A FilePermission object takes two parameters. An example would be the file name (including wildcards, if any) and actions (such as read, write, and/or delete). A permission can act like a macro permission. The implies method on a permission indicates whether or not its permission covers other permissions of the same type.

Permission objects milling around randomly add unwanted chaos to security. PermissionCollection objects group homogeneous permission objects together, making it easier for Java security to find if a permission was granted. PermissionCollection objects also support the implies method, allowing developers to use the object in the same way that a single permission object is consulted. Permissions, a subclass of PermissionCollection, group the different PermissionCollection objects together.

Developers can construct a ProtectionDomain object by supplying a CodeSource and PermissionCollection (or Permissions) object. A class belongs to only one ProtectionDomain, and can find the ProtectionDomain that it belongs to by calling its getProtectionDomain() method. The Java program can query the returned ProtectionDomain object to determine the class' CodeSource and granted Permissions.

Upon construction, a ProtectionDomain indicates to the AccessController the set of permissions that are allowed for all classes that are loaded from a CodeSource location. Many Java core classes consult the AccessController class to see if permissions are allowed. For example, Java security won't allow a file read operation without the appropriate FilePermission in the PermissionCollection that's associated with the CodeSource from where the class was loaded.

Checking permissions

A single class performing actions represents the simple case of permission checking. Java security looks to see if the class has the appropriate permission in the PermissionCollection for the ProtectionDomain to which the class belongs. Permission checking becomes more complex when one class calls another. Before Java 2 security allows an action, such as a socket connection to succeed, all the classes on the calling stack are checked to see if the required permission has been granted. Some classes are immune from this query, such as Java core classes or classes in the trusted Java extension directory.

A complex two-class example is shown using the scenario of two friends who live near Antietam creek and who would like to check out a book from the school's library. Ben has a library card and thus has permission to check books out. Although an aspiring reader, Patrick isn't old enough to attend school and doesn't have library privileges. By himself, Ben can check out books, but if Patrick asks Ben to check a book out, Ben won't have permission because Patrick doesn't have permission.

In this example, the Permission to check out library books as a RuntimePermission with "libraryCard" as the parameter name. In a more sophisticated world, we could create a LibraryPermission class as a subclass of BasicPermission. The permission name could be "checkoutBooks" in this extension.

Ben.java and Patrick.java demonstrate this example. Ben's located in package school and Patrick in package preschool. The compiled classes can be placed in separate jar files, school.jar and preschool.jar. Note that Ben.class and Patrick.class have separate ProtectionDomain objects since they exist in separate jar files.

Ben.java

```
package ibm.book.school;

import java.security.*;

public class Ben {
    public static void main(String args[]) {
        RuntimePermission perm = new RuntimePermission("libraryCard");
        Ben.checkPermission(perm);
    }
```

```
    public static void checkPermission(Permission checkperm)
        throws SecurityException{
        try {
            System.out.println("Ben's checking permission.");
            AccessController.checkPermission(checkperm);
            System.out.println("Ben can check out library books.");
        } catch (Exception e) {
            System.out.println("Ben can't check out library books.");
            throw new SecurityException(
                "Can't check out library books.");
        }
    }

    public static void checkPermission2(Permission perm)
        throws SecurityException {
        final Permission checkperm = perm;
        System.out.println(
            "Ben's checking permission with doPrivilege.");
        try {
            AccessController.doPrivileged(
                new PrivilegedExceptionAction() {
                public Object run() {
                    AccessController.checkPermission(checkperm);
                    return null;
                }}
            );
            System.out.println(
                "Ben can check out library books with doPrivilege.");
        } catch (Exception e) {
            System.out.println(
                "Ben can't check out library books with doPrivilege.");
            throw new SecurityException(
                "Can't checkout library books.");
        }
    }
}
```

Patrick.java

```
package ibm.book.preschool;

import java.security.*;
import ibm.book.school.Ben;
```

```
public class Patrick {

    public static void main(String args[]) {
        RuntimePermission perm = new RuntimePermission("libraryCard");

        try {
            System.out.println("Patrick's checking permission.");
            AccessController.checkPermission(perm);
            System.out.println("Patrick can check out library books.");
        } catch (Exception e) {
            System.out.println("Patrick can't check out library books.");
        }

        try {
            System.out.println("\nPatrick asks Ben to check out a book.");
            Ben.checkPermission(perm);
            System.out.println(
                "Patrick can check out a library book through Ben.");
        } catch (Exception e) {
            System.out.println(
                "Patrick can't check out a library book through Ben.");
        }

        try {
            System.out.println(
                "\nPatrick again asks Ben to check out a book.");
            Ben.checkPermission2(perm);
            System.out.println(
                "Patrick finally can check out a library book through Ben.");
        } catch (Exception e) {
            System.out.println(
                "Patrick still can't check out a library book through Ben.");
        }
    }
}
```

The following java.policy entry grants permission for Ben to check out books. The default policy takes the form of a flat ASCII file with stanzas grouping together permissions with no constraints or a URL and/or certificate. Java security reads the permissions from the file and creates Policy objects that get evaluated for each class when its ProtectionDomain is created.

```
grant codeBase "file:c:/example/lib/school.jar" {
    permission java.lang.RuntimePermission "libraryCard";
};
```

After compiling, developers can run the Java interpreter on either class because they both have a main method. When Ben is run by himself, he invokes the AccessController.checkPermission method and succeeds in checking out a book.

When Patrick is run, he tries three ways to check out a book. First, he tries to check out a book by himself and fails. Next, he asks Ben to check out a book using Ben's checkPermission public class method. Ben won't be able to check out a book because his caller, Patrick, doesn't have permission. Lastly, Patrick asks Ben again to check out a book, but this time he succeeds by calling Ben's checkPermission2 public class method.

Patrick output

```
C:\>java ibm.book.preschool.Patrick
Patrick's checking permission.
Patrick can't check out library books.

Patrick asks Ben to check out a book.
Ben's checking permission.
Ben can't check out library books.
Patrick can't check out a library book through Ben.

Patrick again asks Ben to check out a book.
Ben's checking permission with doPrivilege.
Ben can check out library books with doPrivilege.
Patrick finally can check out a library book through Ben.
```

Ben has a way around Patrick's lack of permission to check out books. Ben can state that only he should be checked for permission and that the permissions in Patrick's ProtectionDomain should not be checked. The Ben.checkPermission2 method uses a doPrivileged method that tells Java security not to check his callers for Permission. In this method, Ben asserts that he knows his callers may lack authority to perform the action, and Ben wishes to perform this action on his own authority.

In a more sophisticated world, the Java program wouldn't need to make checks beforehand with AccessController.checkPermission, unless the program wants to precheck if a permission was granted. Instead, Java security or the user's classes that perform the user created action would call the AccessController.checkPermission method before performing the action.

Conclusion

Java 2 security has evolved to a unified permissions model. ProtectionDomain objects exist as dynamic and essential objects in the Java security world. ProtectionDomain objects bring together many different security objects and Java security references these objects when checking permissions. If the doPrivileged block isn't utilized, all non-trusted classes on the stack must have the required permission for the checkPermission to succeed.

Applets and Java security

In response to customer demands for greater control over their enterprise environments, the Java security model has evolved from its divisional model of local and remote trusts to a fine-grained model based on individual permissions. This evolution includes Java applications and applets. With the Java 1.1 security model, applets that were loaded locally, such as through the file protocol, were given greater capabilities than those loaded remotely, such as through the HTTP protocol. With Java 2 security, all local and remote applets must adhere to a Java policy specified by the user or administrator. This article examines how applets can take advantage of the new Java 2 security model.

Why security?

With the Internet and intranets, users can easily access Web sites to view content. Unlike applications, which must be consciously downloaded and run by the user, visited Web sites can contain a variety of Java applets that run automatically. Users could turn off their Web browser's Java Runtime Environment (JRE), but they would lose the capability to run all Java applets. Users and administrators require a customizable middle ground between preventing all Java applets from running and opening up all of the user's resources without restriction.

Applets need security to protect access to many resources, from reading or writing local files to making connections to other sockets. With Java 2 security, users and administrators can specify a policy in which individual permissions indicate what resources and capabilities to those resources an applet can have. In addition, the Java policy can give permissions to applets loaded from a particular codebase, such as a URL to a particular server or signed by a specified certificate.

Java 2 security implements its default policy module with an ASCII policy file that can be optionally loaded from a URL, as defined within the user's Java security file, when the JRE starts. The flexibility of allowing multiple policy files to be specified gives users and administrators the ability to have an enterprise-wide policy that's loaded from a network file system or Web server, as well as a local policy that is stored on the user's local file system.

All permissions within a policy file are considered granted. If a permission has not been explicitly granted, it is denied. Note that Java 2 security grants applets a number of implicit permissions that allow the applet to perform its tasks without impacting the user's environment, such as loading other files—for example, a GIF or WAV file—from the same codebase. Any action that would give the applet access to sensitive information or resources on the user's workstation is not allowed unless granted in the user's Java policy file.

Running applets

The Java 2 platform continues to ship the AppletViewer application, which allows users to load and run applets without a full-blown Web browser. The latest version recognizes that it participates within the Java 2 security realm. It utilizes the JRE to load the Java policy and apply its permissions to govern the resources to which the applet has access.

Although the AppletViewer is available, users are more likely to run applets from the Web browsers they use to navigate the Web. The current versions of these Web browsers are based on the Java 1.1 platform, which means that applets written to take advantage of the new features in the Java 2 architecture cannot run within these browsers. Applets are restricted to the classes and methods implemented by the browser's JRE. The various browsers have their own security models that are different from each other, but also are different from the Java 2 platform. Unlike Java 2 security, the browser's security model is geared to the local user, not to enterprise environments. For example, a permission that one user allows cannot easily be replicated to apply to all users in the enterprise.

The Java plug-in

To allow users to run applets in a different JRE than those shipped with the Web browser, Sun created the Java Plug-in that users can install and configure on their workstations. The Java Plug-in is shipped as part of the Java 2 platform, and its inclusion gives the Java 2 security model a wider audience.

The Java Plug-in allows applets to run in a JRE other than the one supplied with the user's Web browser. With this ability, users can configure the Java Plug-in to run an applet with a Java 2 JRE, or even an older Java 1.1 JRE. The Java Plug-in gives users the capabilities and functionality of the Java 2 platform and its security model without the users needing to wait for the manufacturer to upgrade the JRE shipped with its browser.

In addition to specifying a JRE, the Java Plug-in allows users to specify a number of configuration options, including the command line parameters to pass to the JRE, whether or not to cache jar files and the proxy addresses to use.

The Java Plug-in recognizes that it should run an applet under its configured JRE by HTML tags. Since the browser is in charge of loading the Web page and interpreting its tags, the browser still construes the standard applet tag as a directive to run the applet under the browser's JRE.

With the extendable object tag for the Microsoft Web browsers or embed tag for the Netscape Web browsers that correspond to the original applet tag, the browser knows to run the Java Plug-in and allow it to execute the applet under the user specified JRE. The object or embed tag includes regular applet tag parameters, such as the archive, codebase, code and other parameters specific to the applet. Sun provides an HTML converter tool to help administrators automate the process of converting the applet tags on their existing HTML pages.

Although the Java Plug-in requires enterprise and Web server administrators to change their Web pages, this process has the side benefit of allowing the browser to continue to support applets written for its own JRE. For example, the user could visit a site with a Java 2 applet and next load a new site with an applet written for the browser's JRE. Both would exist with their own JRE, but now the Java 2 applet can run under its enterprise-wide or fine-grained security policy.

Example scenario

The following example demonstrates how Benjamin, a developer with Antietam Software, can run an applet with the Java 2 security model in a Web browser.

First, Ben's Java security file indicates that his policy file exists at a URL location. The policy file includes the following grant statement, indicating that it allows classes loaded from the antietam Web server read access to a file called " c:\appletparms.txt":

```
grant codebase "http://antietam/-" {
    permission java.io.FilePermission "c:\\appletparms.txt", "read";
};
```

Other than the implicit actions provided to applets by the JRE, applets do not have permission to read other files or take other actions unless specifically granted.

Ben would configure his Java Plug-in control panel to run applets under a Java 2 JRE. This can be accomplished by selecting the JRE from a drop-down list of detected JREs or by entering the path to an installed JRE.

The sample applet that reads the contents of the c:\appletparms.txt file is shown in SampleRead.java. If an exception occurs, the applet prints the error and ends.

SampleRead.java

```
package ibm.book;

import java.applet.*;
import java.awt.*;
import java.io.*;

public class SampleRead extends Applet {
  public void init() {
    TextArea textArea = new TextArea();
    String filename = "c:\\appletparms.txt";
    String line;
    try {
      super.init();
      setSize(400, 200);
      setLayout(new BorderLayout());
      add(textArea, BorderLayout.CENTER);
      textArea.append("contents of " + filename + ":");
      File f = new File(filename);
      BufferedReader br = new BufferedReader(new FileReader(f));
      line = br.readLine();
      while (line != null) {
          textArea.append("\r\n"+line);
          line = br.readLine();
        }
      textArea.append("\r\nEOF");
    }
    catch (Exception e) {
      line = "** Exception:  " + e.toString();
      textArea.append("\n"+line);
    }
  }
}
```

This applet is available on the antietam Web server in the readparms.html file. Normally, the applet tag would define how the applet was sized and run, but for use with the Java Plug-in, the readparms.html file was converted to utilize the object and embed tags. The Microsoft Web browser knows how to interpret the object tag and the Netscape Web browser, how to understand the embed tag. Since browsers ignore tags that they do not recognize, the Microsoft Web browser ignores the embed tag and its parameters. The Netscape Web browser ignores the object tag.

With the applet and HTML file on the Web server and the c:\appletparms.txt file on the Ben's workstation, when Ben accesses the readparms.html file, the browser runs the applet under the specified Java 2 JRE. Because the applet was granted read access to the c:\appletparms.txt file, it shows the contents of the file in the Web browser. If Ben removes the FilePermission from the policy file, the Java 2 runtime throws an AccessControlException when the applet tries to open the file and the applet displays an error message.

Conclusion

The Java 2 security model does not apply just to Java applications. Java applets can exploit the functionality of the Java 2 platform as well. The Java Plug-in makes it easy for users to run applets written to different JREs within their existing Netscape and Microsoft Web browsers.

Implementing custom security permissions in Java security

The Java security model has been undergoing an evolution as rapid and as radical as the Java language itself. In the span of a few short years, Java security has evolved from the sandbox model through a binary trust model to the now fine-grained, policy-driven, extensible Java 2 model. Application writers may have had some amount of difficulty in keeping up with the changes. This article examines how application writers can exploit the new Java 2 security model and implement custom security protection for their programs.

Why permissions?

Before diving into the details of how one develops custom security permissions in Java 2 security, it is worth spending a few moments discussing the need for this activity. What has already been accomplished in the Java architecture itself, and what are the responsibilities of application writers? Java 2 security provides a fine-grained, policy-driven, extensible security model. Java security now helps protect system resources with internal policy checks and offers some interesting permission classes that may be extended by application writers. Java security also externalizes the security policy so that it can be amended to allow programs to run, but run with a minimum set of necessary permissions. However, application writers still need to add security checks into their own code before accessing their own resources.

Java 2 security provides interesting permission classes for use and extension. It can allow custom permissions to be specified in policy files, and it helps protect the system from rogue programs. However, it cannot automatically secure an application. That is up to the developer. As application writers enrich the Java platform with more and more high-quality programs, however, protecting the value that they provide with security checks becomes advantageous. Enterprise customers demand such sophistication.

Building blocks

Java 2 security has a number of Permission classes. Most of them are used internally in the Java API, but there are a few that can be used "as is" or extended for use by a developer. Permissions actually have two faces. A permission entry in a policy file, like the one shown in the code snippet below,

```
permission   ibm.book.WeirdPermission   "MrFeathers", "open mail";
```

represents an actual permission granted to a class. A permission object like the one shown below allows you to ask if you actually have a specific permission:

```
AccessController.checkPermission
      (new ibm.book.WeirdPermission("MrFeathers ", "open mail"));
```

Permissions may have one or more optional actions, like the "open mail" action above. The semantics of these actions are entirely up to the implementer of the permission class.

The parent of all Permission classes is the abstract class java.security.Permission. All other permissions must extend this class or one of its subclasses. The signature of the AccessController.checkPermission() method is that it takes a Permission object as a parameter. Because the AccessController is the workhorse class of the Java 2 security framework, if users can't meet the interface, they are out of the security game. The Permission class has an abstract equals() method, which is intended to allow you to test for strict equality, as you might expect. The real heart of the security engine is the abstract implies() method.

The AccessController does not check for strict equality, but rather that the program possesses a permission that implies that it can perform the operation it is attempting.

Permissions have a name that identifies the specific object to which the permission relates. Permissions may have actions associated with them, and whether they do or not, every permission class is required to have two constructors: one that simply takes a name, and one that takes a name and some actions. This latter constructor is driven by some implementation details and does not require that permissions actually support actions. If this seems particularly opaque, the example program that follows may shed some light.

A very useful class is java.security.BasicPermission. Although it is abstract, it has no abstract methods and it implements all of the abstract methods of the Permission class. Being able to extend BasicPermission saves a certain amount of programming. BasicPermission objects don't have actions (hence the name!), but do implement wildcard behavior in their names. Their names are treated as hierarchical, following a dot-separated annotation.

For example, to extend the previous example, we might follow the convention that the layout of the permission name would always be network.show.role.name. So, we might have mystation.MyShow.characters.MrFeathers, mystation.MyShow.characters.PoMiester, mystation.MyShow.writers.IMConfused, and so on. These permissions could still be specified by their (now longer) full name, or they could be specified with an asterisk wildcard character: mystation.* that would match each of these, no matter what the depth. Specifying simply an asterisk would match every single possible BasicPermission. Wildcard behavior is limited as follows: Partial names are not supported, such as mystation.My*, and the wildcard must be on the right (no *.characters.*).

Example program

Given this background, it's easy to see that with proper construction of the permission namespace, it is a very simple job to implement custom permission. If the permission namespace can be laid out such that the wildcard present in the BasicPermission class works, all that needs to be done to implement custom permissions is to extend the BasicPermission class as shown in the simple WeirdPermission.java.

Simple WeirdPermission.java

```
package ibm.book;

public class WeirdPermission extends BasicPermission {
    public WeirdPermission(String name) {
        super(name);
    }
    public WeirdPermission(String name, String action) {
        super(name,action);
    }
}
```

And that's it. The developer picks up all the function that BasicPermission offers, including the wild-card behavior. Now that the developer has subclassed the class, features beyond those provided by BasicPermission can be added. For example, the developer might be required to support single-character, anywhere-in-the-string wildcards. The developer probably still wants to extend BasicPermission, so that other behaviors embodied in that class can be inherited. The work is relatively easy, as shown in the extended WeirdPermission.java.

Extended WeirdPermission.java

```
package ibm.book;
import java.security.*;

public final class WeirdPermission extends BasicPermission {
    private transient boolean wild;
        public WeirdPermission(String name) {
            super(name);
            init(name);
        }
        public WeirdPermission(String name, String action) {
            super(name); //ignore actions
            init(name);
        }
        public boolean implies(Permission permission) {
            if (permission == null || !(permission instanceof
                WeirdPermission))
                return false;
            WeirdPermission wp = (WeirdPermission) permission;
            String thisName = getName();
            String thatName = wp.getName();
            if (thisName.equals(thatName)) return true;
            // now know names don't exactly match
            boolean thisWild = isWild();
            boolean thatWild = wp.isWild();
            // if no wildcard, no possibility for a match
            if (!thisWild && !thatWild) return false;
            // do not permit both to have wildcards, simplifies example
            if (thisWild && thatWild) return false;
            // check for match on length
            if (thisName.length() != thatName.length()) return false;
            if (thatWild) { //wp has a wildcard
                return parseWild(thatName,thisName);
            } else {
                return parseWild(thisName,thatName);
            }
        }
        private void init(String name) {
            int index = name.indexOf("?");
            if (index == -1) { // no wildcard
                wild = false;
            } else { //Have at least one wildcard
                wild = true;
            }
```

```
    } // end of init
    public boolean isWild() {
        return wild;
    }
    private boolean parseWild(String wildThing, String tameThing) {
        int wildIndex = wildThing.indexOf("?");
        if (! (wildThing.substring(0,wildIndex).equals(
            tameThing.substring(0,wildIndex)))) return false;

        //OK, know it matched up to wildcard
        //Look for exact match afterwards
        if (wildThing.length() == wildIndex+1) return true; // done
        if (wildThing.substring(wildIndex+1).equals(
            tameThing.substring(wildIndex+1))) return true;
        else return false;
    }
}
```

TestPermission.java instantiates two instances of WeirdPermission and demonstrates the new wild-card behavior in the implies method. Note that this example focuses on the naming given to the permission instance. If you wanted to support actions on the permission object, additional modifications would be required.

TestPermission.java

```
package ibm.book;

import java.security.*;

public class TestPermission {
    public static void main(String args[]) {
        WeirdPermission t1 = new
            WeirdPermission("mystation.MyShow.characters.MrFeathers");
        WeirdPermission t2 = new
            WeirdPermission("mystation.MyShow.characters.MrFeathers");
        if (t1.implies(t2)) {
            System.out.println("First one worked");
        } else {
            System.out.println("First one failed");
        }
        t2 = new
```

```
        WeirdPermission("mystation.MyShow.characters.M?Feathers");
    if (t1.implies(t2)) {
        System.out.println("Second one worked");
    } else {
        System.out.println("Second one failed");
    }
  }
}
```

Conclusion

Java 2 security represents a real advance in the area of security. Some of the advantages accrue to everyone using the Java platform, without effort on their part; but application developers must exert some effort to ensure that their programs protect their resources from misuse. The Java 2 platform provides some useful building blocks for use by developers, and it is often possible to slightly modify these building block classes for immediate reuse. Reusing or extending an extant implementation allows leverage of Java technologies for maximum productivity, but constrains flexibility.

Introduction to Cryptography

In this section, we provide a discussion of the fundamentals of cryptography through a series of articles and explore more advanced topics, such as implementing your own cryptographic provider. The "Choosing" article also gives you advice on how to select the best cryptography for your e-business deployment.

- Java cryptography Part 1: Encryption and decryption

- Java cryptography Part 2: Key generation and management

- Java cryptography Part 3: Implementing your own provider

- Java cryptography Part 4: JCE export considerations

- Choosing the right cryptography for your e-business application

Java cryptography Part 1: Encryption and decryption

Beginning with Version 1.1 of Sun's Java Development Kit (JDK), general purpose APIs for cryptographic functions, collectively known as the Java Cryptography Architecture (JCA), are provided along with its extension, the Java Cryptography Extension (JCE). The Java 2 Standard Development Kit (SDK) significantly enhances the Java Cryptography Architecture. Specifically, the Java 2 SDK augments the certificate management infrastructure to support X.509 V3 certificates.

Note: The Java Development Kits (JDKs) are referred to as Standard Development Kits (SDKs) in the Java 2 platform.

This article describes the basic classes used in encryption and decryption and how to create a simple program exploiting these features.

United States export considerations

The security classes shipped with the Java 2 Standard Development Kit provide for only the message digest and digital signature part of the cryptographic spectrum. This allows you to perform reliable authentication that, in turn, can be used as a basis for implementing access controls that relax the sandbox restrictions. However, the Java Cryptography Architecture alone does not provide the general-purpose encryption functionality needed to send confidential data.

This function is provided by the JCE, which is an extension to the cryptography-related classes shipped with the Java 2 SDK from Sun. JCE uses the same structure as the JCA, being composed of engine classes that expose the algorithms in a generic way. The JCE provides engine classes for (a)symmetric-key encryption and for generating and manipulating the secret keys that such algorithms require.

The primary principle in the design of the JCA has been to separate the cryptographic concepts from their algorithmic implementations. The separation of the encryption classes satisfied the United States Export requirements in effect at the time it was developed and allows the SDK with the JCA to be freely distributed, while restricting the distribution of the JCE. Before we explain how JCA achieves this separation, it is worthwhile to review the types of classes supplied by the Java 2 SDK, the APIs that are part of the JCA and the API extensions supplied by the JCE.

We will learn later in this section how changes in the United States Export laws and in the design of JCE currently allow JCE to be exported.

Java 2 SDK, JCA and JCE APIs relationship

The Java 2 SDK APIs consist of core classes that are shipped with the Java Virtual Machine (JVM). The set of core classes in the Java 2 platform can be divided into two subsets:

- Security-related core classes

- Other core classes

The security-related core classes can be further subdivided as:

- Access control and permission related core classes

- Cryptography-related core classes

Of these, only the cryptography-related core classes are part of the JCA APIs. The JCE extends the JCA API to include APIs for encryption, key exchange, and Message Authentication Code (MAC). Together, the JCE and the cryptography aspects of the Java 2 SDK provide a platform-independent cryptography API. The JCE is released separately as an extension to the Java 2 SDK, in accordance with current United States export control regulations.

Java Cryptography Extension 1.2

JCE has been provided as an extension to the Java platform. Sun's JCE 1.2 provides a framework and implementation for encryption, key generation, key agreement, and MAC to supplement the interfaces and implementations of message digests and digital signatures provided by Java 2 SDK, Standard Edition, V1.2.

The provider architecture of the JCA aims to allow algorithm independence. The design principles behind JCE also share the same philosophy of implementation and algorithm independence by the use of the provider architecture. In addition to making it possible to use newer algorithms for generating keys, JCE also introduces some very new interfaces and classes that facilitate the implementation of these concepts.

JCE provides a framework for encryption, (session) key generation and key agreement, and MAC algorithms. Support for encryption includes symmetric, asymmetric, block, stream, and future ciphers.

Provider and the packages

The IBMJCE and SunJCE providers each consist of the main package javax.crypto and its two sub-packages javax.crypto.spec and javax.crypto.interfaces.

The javax.crypto package forms the main body of the JCE 1.2 class structure. The package primarily consists of classes that represent the new concepts of ciphers, key agreements, and message authentication codes and their corresponding SPI classes.

The javax.crypto.spec package consists of various key specification and algorithm parameter specification classes.

The javax.crypto.interfaces package consists of the DHKey interface and a couple of its subinterfaces —DHPrivateKey and DHPublicKey. These are the interfaces for the keys based on the Diffie-Hellman algorithms.

The Cipher Class

The javax.crypto.Cipher engine class forms the core of the JCE 1.2 framework. This class provides the functionality of a cryptographic cipher used for encryption and decryption.

Like other engine classes, the Cipher class is instantiated using its getInstance() factory method. This method takes as argument a String object that represents a transformation. A transformation is a string that describes the operation (or set of operations) to be performed on the given input, to produce some output. A transformation always includes the name of a cryptographic algorithm (for example, Data Encryption Standard or DES), which may be followed by a feedback mode and padding scheme:

A Cipher object obtained from getInstance() must be initialized for either encryption or decryption mode. These modes are defined as final integer constants in the Cipher class. The two modes can be referenced by their symbolic names ENCRYPT_MODE and DECRYPT_MODE.

Algorithms usually operate on blocks having a predefined size. Plain text packets, which are of a length not a multiple of that size, must be padded prior to encrypting according to a specified padding scheme.

From what we said, a transformation is of the form algorithm/mode/padding or algorithm. If mode and padding are not specified, provider-specific default values are used.

For example, the following is a valid way to create a Cipher object:

```
Cipher c = Cipher.getInstance("DES/CBC/PKCS5Padding");
```

Optionally, getInstance() can accept, as a second argument, the name of the provider after the transformation parameter.

A Cipher object is initialized by calling the init() method. When this happens, it loses all previously acquired states. In other words, initializing a Cipher is equivalent to creating a new instance of that Cipher and initializing it.

Data can be encrypted or decrypted in one step (single-part operation) or in multiple steps (multiple-part operation). You will encrypt or decrypt data in a single step or in multiple steps depending on whether you call the doFinal() or update() method, respectively. A multiple-part operation is useful if the exact length of the data is not known in advance, or if the data is too long to be stored in memory all at once.

The Cipher stream classes

JCE 1.2 introduces the concept of secure streams, which combine an InputStream or OutputStream with a Cipher object. The CipherInputStream and CipherOutputStream classes provide secure streams:

(1)   The javax.crypto.CipherInputStream class is a FilterInputStream that encrypts or decrypts the data passing through it. It is composed of an InputStream, or one of its subclasses, and a Cipher. CipherInputStream represents a secure input stream into which a Cipher object has been interposed.   The read methods of CipherInputStream return data that are read from the underlying InputStream but have additionally been processed by the embedded Cipher object.

Notice that the Cipher object must be fully initialized before being used by a CipherInputStream. For example, if the embedded Cipher has been initialized for decryption, the CipherInputStream will attempt to decrypt the data it reads from the underlying InputStream before returning it to the application.

(2)   The javax.crypto.CipherOutputStream class is a FilterOutputStream that encrypts or decrypts the data passing through it. It is composed of an OutputStream, or one of its subclasses, and a Cipher. CipherOutputStream represents a secure output stream into which a Cipher object has been interposed. The write methods of CipherOutputStream first process the data with the embedded Cipher object before writing it out to the underlying OutputStream.

The Cipher object must be fully initialized before being used by a CipherOutputStream. For example, if the embedded Cipher has been initialized for encryption, the CipherOutputStream will encrypt its data, before writing it out to the underlying output stream.

Sample program using the JCE 1.2 APIs to encrypt and decrypt

The following listing shows a simple program, EncryptDecrypt.java, that reads data from an input file; encrypts it using a Cipher object, jcecipher1, initialized for the DES algorithm in the ENCRYPT_MODE; decrypts it using another Cipher object, jcecipher2, initialized for the DES algorithm in the DECRYPT_MODE; and then prints the output to a file.

EncryptDecrypt.java

```
package ibm.book;

import java.io.*;
import java.security.*;
import javax.crypto.*;

public class EncryptDecrypt {

    public static void main(String args[]) {

      if (args.length != 2) {
        System.out.println(
            "Usage: java EncryptDecrypt inputFileName outputFileName");
      } else {
        try {
```

```
// generate Cipher objects for encoding and decoding
Cipher itsocipher1 = Cipher.getInstance("DES");
Cipher itsocipher2 = Cipher.getInstance("DES");

// generate a KeyGenerator object
KeyGenerator KG = KeyGenerator.getInstance("DES");
System.out.println("Using algorithm " + KG.getAlgorithm());

// generate a DES key
Key mykey = KG.generateKey();

// initialize the Cipher objects
System.out.println("Initializing ciphers...");
itsocipher1.init(Cipher.ENCRYPT_MODE, mykey);
itsocipher2.init(Cipher.DECRYPT_MODE, mykey);

// creating the encrypting cipher stream
System.out.println("Creating the encrypting cipher stream...");
FileInputStream fis = new FileInputStream(args[0]);
CipherInputStream cis1 = new CipherInputStream(fis, itsocipher1);

// creating the decrypting cipher stream
System.out.println("Creating the decrypting cipher stream...");
CipherInputStream cis2 = new CipherInputStream(cis1, itsocipher2);

// writing the decrypted data to output file
System.out.println(
    "Writing the decrypted data to output file " + args[1]);
FileOutputStream fos = new FileOutputStream(args[1]);
byte[] b2 = new byte[1024];
int i2 = cis2.read(b2);
while (i2 != -1) {
  fos.write(b2, 0, i2);
  i2 = cis2.read(b2);
}
fos.close();
cis1.close();
cis2.close();
} catch (Exception e) {
System.out.println("Caught exception: " + e);
}
  }
 }
}
```

The output file name also is specified on the command line. Use the following command to compile:

```
javac EncryptDecrypt.java
```

For the above command to work, the IBMJCE or SunJCE provider must be installed on your system. Make sure your CLASSPATH environment includes the JCE classes.

Then launch the program, passing on the command line the name of an existing input text file, jce.txt, and the name of an output file where the EncryptDecrypt program writes the data that it has encrypted and decrypted:

```
java ibm.book.EncryptDecrypt jce.txt jce_out.txt
```

To check the results, open the jce_out.txt file with a text editor, and verify that its contents are exactly the same as the contents of the original file jce.txt.

Conclusion

Java 2 security-related classes are divided between those available with the SDKs and the JCE. The JCE includes classes that extend the Java Cryptography Architecture and allow pluggable cryptographic classes. With the JCE, developers can harness the power of encryption in their applications.

Java cryptography Part 2: Key generation and management

This article continues our discussion of Java cryptography and describes some of the key generation and management classes used in advanced encryption and decryption and how to create a program exploiting these features.

Secret key interfaces and classes

JCE 1.2 from Sun offers a set of classes and interfaces to manage secret keys. Also known as symmetric or private keys, secret keys are used at both ends of the cryptographic process. The secret key that encrypts contents also can be used to decrypt the encrypted contents.

- The javax.crypto.SecretKey interface contains no methods or constants. Its only purpose is to group and provide type safety for secret keys. Provider implementations of this interface must overwrite the equals() and hashCode() methods inherited from java.lang.Object, so that secret keys are compared based on their underlying key material and not based on reference. Since it extends the Key interface, this interface is an opaque representation of a symmetric key.

- The javax.crypto.SecretKeyFactory class represents a factory for secret keys. Key factories are bi-directional, which means that they allow building of an opaque Key object from a given key specification (key material) or retrieving the underlying key material of a Key object in a suitable format.

In general, key factories are used to convert keys (opaque cryptographic keys of type Key) into key specifications (transparent representations of the underlying key material) and vice versa. In particular, secret key factories operate only on secret keys.

The javax.crypto.spec.SecretKeySpec class specifies a secret key in a provider-independent fashion. It can be used to construct a SecretKey from a byte array, without the need to go through a provider-based SecretKeyFactory. This class is useful only for raw secret keys that can be represented as a byte array and have no key parameters associated with them, for example DES or Triple DES keys. This class is a transparent representation of a secret key.

The KeyGenerator class

The java.security.KeyPairGenerator class, which is part of Sun's Java 2 SDK, Standard Edition, V1.2 APIs, is used to generate a pair of public and private keys. Key pairs differ from secret keys in that one key is used to decrypt the encrypted data stream or vice versa. JCE 1.2 provides for a KeyGenerator engine class that is used to generate secret keys for symmetric algorithms. KeyGenerator objects are created using the getInstance() factory method of the KeyGenerator class. Notice that a factory method is by definition static.

The getInstance() method takes as its argument the name of a symmetric algorithm for which a secret key is to be generated. Optionally, a provider name may be specified. If just an algorithm name is specified, the system will determine if there is an implementation of the requested key generator available in the environment and, if there is more than one, the preferred one will be selected. If both an algorithm name and a package provider are specified, the system will determine if there is an implementation of the requested key generator from the requested provider and throw an exception if there is not. A key generator for a particular symmetric-key algorithm creates a symmetric key that can be used with that algorithm. It also associates algorithm-specific parameters (if any) with the generated key.

The KeyAgreement class

Whenever two or more parties decide to initiate a secure conversation over a non-secure communication channel, they need to use the same secret key (which is called the session key), without transmitting it in the clear over the channel. To achieve this, public-key encryption could be used to transmit the session key securely.

Alternatively, another solution is to use key agreement. A key agreement is a protocol that allows two or more parties to calculate the same secret value without exchanging it directly. Therefore, the parties share the same secret key and can encrypt the communication using symmetric encryption. The most famous of these protocols is the Diffie-Hellman (DH) algorithm, an implementation of which is provided by Sun in JCE 1.2 reference implementation.

The javax.crypto.KeyAgreement class provides the functionality of a key agreement protocol. The keys involved in establishing a shared secret key are created by one of the key generators (KeyPairGenerator or KeyGenerator), a key factory, or as a result from an intermediate phase of the key agreement protocol.

Each party involved in the key agreement has to create a KeyAgreement object. This can be done using the getInstance() factory method of the KeyAgreement class. This method accepts as its argument a string representing a key agreement algorithm as parameter. As with the KeyGenerator class, you can specify a provider as the second argument.

If the Diffie-Hellman algorithm is used, a Diffie-Hellman private key is used to initialize the KeyAgreement object. Additional initialization information may contain a source of randomness and/or a set of algorithm parameters.

Every key agreement protocol consists of a number of phases that need to be executed by each party involved in the key agreement. The doPhase() method is used to execute the next phase in the key agreement. This method takes two arguments: a Key and a boolean.

- The Key argument contains the key to be processed by that phase. In most cases, this is the public key of one of the other parties involved in the key agreement or an intermediate key that was generated by a previous phase. The doPhase() method may return an intermediate key that you may have to send to the other parties of this key agreement, so they can process it in a subsequent phase.

- The boolean parameter specifies whether or not the phase to be executed is the last one in the key agreement.

- A value of false indicates that this is not the last phase of the key agreement and there are more phases to follow.

- A value of true indicates that this is the last phase of the key agreement and the key agreement is completed.

After each party has executed all of the required key agreement phases, the secret key can be computed by calling the generateSecret() method.

Practical example of Java Cryptography

This section describes a couple of examples of the kinds of applications for which the JCA can be used.

In Part 1 of this Java cryptography article series, we provided an example where a text file in the same class was encrypted and then decrypted. Real-life situations are more complex. A realistic situation would be when two persons are situated at two different locations and want to exchange data safely by encrypting the data during transmission. In this situation, there are two different programs for encryption and decryption.

Cryptography scenario

In the first example, consider the following scenario. Bob and Alice, want to exchange data. Bob wants to send data to Alice and wants to encrypt the data to maintain its safety in transit. He writes a program called Encrypt1.java, which does the following:

1.   Reads data from a text file JavaTeam.txt.

2.   Encrypts the data using a Cipher object initialized by the DES algorithm and a DES secret symmetric key.

3.   Stores the encrypted data in a file bob.enc.

4.   Stores the secret key in another file bob.key.

The file JavaTeam.txt read and encrypted by the Encrypt1 Java program:

```
Anthony Nadalin
Theodore Shrader
Bruce Rich
```

Bob runs his program and then sends Alice the two files bob.enc and bob.key. Alice, at the receiving end, writes a program named Decrypt1.java that does the following:

1.   Reads the data from the encrypted file bob.enc.

2.   Reads the key from the bob.key file.

3.   Initiates a Cipher object using this key and decrypts the data from bob.enc.

4.   Writes the decrypted data into a file bob.dec.

Bob's program

Bob's program, called Encrypt1.java, is shown as follows:

Encrypt1.java

```
package ibm.book;

import java.io.*;
import java.security.*;
import javax.crypto.*;


public class Encrypt1 {

    public static void main(String args[]) {

        if (args.length != 3) {
            System.out.println(
                "Usage: java Encrypt1 inputFileName encryptedFilekeyFile");
        } else {
          try {
            // generate a Cipher object
            Cipher jcecipher = Cipher.getInstance("DES/ECB/NoPadding");

            // generate a KeyGenerator object
            KeyGenerator KG = KeyGenerator.getInstance("DES");

            // generate a DES key
            SecretKey mykey = KG.generateKey();

            // initialize the Cipher object to encrypt mode
            jcecipher.init(Cipher.ENCRYPT_MODE, mykey);

            // accessing the input file
            FileInputStream fis = new FileInputStream(args[0]);
            BufferedInputStream bis =new BufferedInputStream(fis);
            int len = bis.available();
            // Make the buffer a multiple of eight bytes for the cipher.
            int modlen = len % 8;
            int newlen = len + (8-modlen);
            byte[] buff = new byte[newlen];
            byte[] encText = new byte[newlen];
```

```
// update the cipher with the data to be encrypted
while (bis.available() != 0) {
    bis.read(buff);
    int bytecount = jcecipher.update(buff, 0, newlen, encText);
}
bis.close();
fis.close();
jcecipher.doFinal();

// write the output file containing the encrypted data
FileOutputStream encfile = new FileOutputStream(args[1]);
encfile.write(encText);
encfile.close();

// write the encoded key to a file
FileOutputStream keyfile = new FileOutputStream(args[2]);
keyfile.write(mykey.getEncoded());

String s1 = mykey.getFormat();
keyfile.close();
} catch (Exception e) {
    System.out.println("Caught Exception: " + e);
}
            }
        }
    }
```

Bob issues the javac command to compile this program.

```
java Encrypt1.java
```

Next, Bob launches it by passing the names of the following files on the command line:

1.   The input file that he wants to encrypt.

2.   The output file containing the encrypted data.

3.   The output file containing the encoded key.

This is the full command launched by Bob:

```
java ibm.book.Encrypt1 JavaTeam.txt bob.enc bob.key
```

The program runs successfully and two files are generated: the file bob.enc containing the encrypted data and the file bob.key containing the encoded key.

Alice's program

Alice receives the two files bob.enc and bob.key and wants to decrypt the encrypted data contained in bob.enc using the key contained in bob.key. For this reason, she writes a program that retrieves the key from the bob.key file, uses the key to initialize a Cipher object and uses the Cipher object to decrypt the message contained in the file bob.enc. The decrypted message is stored in a file called bob.dec.

Alice's program, called Decrypt1.java, is shown as follows.

Decrypt1.java

```
package ibm.book;

import java.io.*;
import java.security.*;
import javax.crypto.*;
import javax.crypto.spec.*;

class Decrypt1 {

    public static void main(String args[]) {
      if (args.length != 3)
        System.out.println(
           "Usage: java Decrypt1 inputEncryptedFile keyFile outputFile");
      else
        try {
            // get the key to decrypt
            FileInputStream kfis = new FileInputStream(args[1]);
            byte[] encKey = new byte[kfis.available()];
            kfis.read(encKey);
            kfis.close();
            SecretKeyFactory mykeyfac1=SecretKeyFactory.getInstance("DES");
            DESKeySpec dk = new DESKeySpec(encKey);
            SecretKey mykey1 = mykeyfac1.generateSecret(dk);

            // generate a Cipher object
            Cipher jceCipher = Cipher.getInstance("DES/ECB/NoPadding");
```

```
            // initialize the Cipher object to decrypt mode
            jceCipher.init(Cipher.DECRYPT_MODE, mykey1);

            // access the file to be decrypted
            FileInputStream data = new FileInputStream(args[0]);
            BufferedInputStream bis = new BufferedInputStream(data);
            int len1 = bis.available();
            byte[] encText1 = new byte[len1];
            byte[] buff = new byte[len1];

            // update the cipher with the data to be decrypted
            while (bis.available() != 0) {
               len1 = bis.read(buff);
               int countjlt = jceCipher.update(buff, 0, len1, encText1);
            }

            bis.close();
            data.close();
            jceCipher.doFinal();

            // write the output file containing the decrypted data
            FileOutputStream encfile = new FileOutputStream(args[2]);
            encfile.write(encText1);
            encfile.close();
         } catch (Exception e) {
            System.out.println("Caught Exception: " + e);
         }
      }
   }
}
```

Alice compiles the program above with javac.

```
      java Decrypt1.java
```

Then she launches the program by passing the following file names on the command line:

1.   The encrypted file to be decrypted.

2.   The file containing Bob's key.

3.   The output file where the decrypted data must be saved

This is the full command launched by Alice:

```
java ibm.book.Decrypt1 bob.enc bob.key bob.dec
```

The program executes successfully and as a result it produces the bob.dec file, containing the decrypted text. On opening bob.dec with a text editor, it shows the same contents as the file JavaTeam.txt. Using Bob's key, Alice has successfully decrypted the message sent by Bob. This example showed the encrypted contents and secret key being accessible from the same location. Typically, the secret key is not sent with the encrypted contents. Instead, Alice and Bob would exchange the key through some secure means or Alice and Bob would use a key agreement protocol.

Conclusion

The JCE includes classes that extend the Java Cryptography Architecture and allows developers to design and implement advanced cryptography techniques. Developers can choose from a variety of key types, including secret keys, key pairs and keys generated through key agreement protocols.

Java cryptography Part 3: Implementing your own provider

This article continues our discussion of Java cryptography and describes the various tasks a developer must complete to write a JCE 1.2 provider.

Implementing your own provider

Each provider installed on the Java Virtual Machine (JVM) supplies implementations of various cryptographic services. The default providers that come with Sun's Java 2 SDK, Standard Edition, V1.2 and JCE 1.2 are SUN and SunJCE respectively. Note that only when JCE 1.2 is installed can the JCE-specific implementations supplied by the provider be accessed. JCE implementations include those services under export control, such as cipher algorithms.

Clients may configure their Java Runtime Environments (JREs) with different providers and specify a preference order for each of them. The different implementations can vary. They may be software or hardware based and might be platform dependent or independent. If you wish to use your own algorithms, you need to create your own provider supplying cryptographic service implementations. To implement a provider, you need to do a number of things, as explained in the following sections.

Write the Service Implementation code

First you need to write the code that supplies algorithm-specific implementations of the cryptographic services you are providing. The type of the service can be:

- Cipher algorithms
- Key Agreement algorithms
- Key Factories
- Key (Pair) Generators
- MAC algorithms

- Secret Key Factories

- Signature algorithms

- Message digests

- (Pseudo-)Random number generation algorithms

- Certificate Factories

- KeyStores

- Algorithm parameter management

- Algorithm parameter generation services

For each cryptographic service, you need to create a subclass of the appropriate Service Provider Interface (SPI) class. In the subclass, you need to:

- Supply implementations for the abstract methods, whose names usually begin with engine.

- Ensure there is a public constructor without any arguments.

When a service is requested, the JVM looks up the subclass implementing that service. The JVM then creates the Class object associated with the subclass and creates an instance of the subclass by calling the newInstance() method for that Class object. The newInstance() method requires a class to have a public constructor without any parameters. A default constructor without any arguments is automatically generated when a class does not have any constructors. If a class defines any other constructors, a public constructor without any arguments must be explicitly implemented.

Give the provider a name

This short step is important, so that applications can specify this provider by name. In this article, "My Provider," abbreviated "MYJCE," was used for our provider name.

Write a master class

Next, create a subclass of the java.security.Provider class. The subclass should be a final class, and its constructor should call super(), specifying the provider name, version number and a string detailing information about the provider and algorithms it supports. For example:

```
private static String info =
        "MY Provider implements the following: \r\n" +
    "Cipher algorithms  :   Mars, Seal\r\n";
public MYJCE() {
        super("MYJCE", 1.0, info);
}
```

In the above example, our name is MYJCE, the version number is 1.0 and the rest is the information about the provider. This information can be retrieved by the applications using the Provider.getInfo() method.

For each service implemented by the provider, there must be a property whose name is the type of service, followed by a period and the name of the algorithm, certificate type or keystore type to which the service applies. The JCA services include:

- Signature

- MessageDigest

- KeyPairGenerator

- SecureRandom

- KeyFactory

- KeyStore

- CertificateFactory

- AlgorithmParameterGenerator

- AlgorithmParameters

The property value must specify the fully qualified name of the class implementing the service. If you are implementing a provider for the JCE 1.2, then the type of service also can be:

- Cipher

- KeyAgreement

- KeyGenerator

- Mac

- SecretFactory

For example, a provider that implements the MARS Cipher algorithm in a class named MARS, found in the com.my.security.provider, has the following statement:

```
put("Cipher.Mars", "com.my.crypto.provider.Mars");
```

If the cryptographic service is Cipher, the name of the algorithm may actually represent a transformation and may be composed of an algorithm name, a particular operation mode and a padding scheme. For example, RSA/ECB/PKCS1Padding indicates RSA algorithm, ECB operation mode and PKCS1 padding.

In general, a transformation is of the form algorithm/mode/padding or simply algorithm. A provider may supply a separate class for each combination of algorithm/mode/padding, or may decide to provide more generic classes representing sub-transformations corresponding to algorithm or algorithm/mode or algorithm//padding. in this case, the requested mode and padding are set automatically by the getInstance() methods of Cipher, which invokes the engineSetMode() and engineSetPadding() methods of the provider's subclass of CipherSpi.

A Cipher property in a provider master class may have one of the following formats:

- Cipher.algName for implementing algName with pluggable mode and padding

- Cipher.algName/mode for implementing algName in the specified mode, with pluggable padding

- Cipher.algName//padding for implementing algName with the specified padding, with pluggable mode

- Cipher.algName/mode/padding implementing algName with the specified mode and padding

Notice that the double backslash (//) means no mode is specified, only the algorithm and the padding is specified. If you say algName/padding, the provider takes the padding to be a mode.

Compile the code

Of course, the code written needs to be compiled. You can create a ZIP or a JAR file after producing your class files.

Install and configure the provider

The provider code produced must be installed and configured for the Java 2 SDK platform to recognize.

There are two ways to install your provider on your system. To statically add your provider, edit the java.security file found in the lib/security directory underneath the SDK installation directory. You need to add the following line:

```
Security.provider.n=com.my.security.crypto.Provider
```

Note the "n" indicates the order of the provider in your configuration file and the order that the providers are searched by the JVM. If you want to write an application that uses your new provider, but you do not want to have to modify the java.security file, use the following code:

```
java.security.Provider p = new com.my.security.crypto.Provider();
Security.addProvider(p);
```

Test if the provider is ready

The best way to test if the provider is ready is to write a small program that attempts to find the provider and test if the algorithms are available.

Algorithm aliases

For many cryptographic algorithms, there is a single official standard name. For example, DESede is the standard name for the triple DES cipher algorithm. This enables clients to use aliases when referring to algorithms, rather than their standard names. For example, the MYJCE provider's master class, called MYJCE itself, defines the alias 3DES for the cipher algorithm whose standard name is DESede. Thus, the following statements are equivalent:

```
Cipher ca = Cipher.getInstance("DESede", "MYJCE");
Cipher ca = Cipher.getInstance("3DES", "MYJCE");
```

Aliases can be defined in the master class. To define an alias, you have to create a property named Alg.Alias.engineClassName.aliasName, where engineClassName is specified as Signature, MessageDigest, KeyPairGenerator, KeyFactory, AlgorithmParameterGenerator or AlgorithmParameters, and aliasName is the alias name you define. The value of the property must be the standard algorithm name for the algorithm for which you are defining an alias.

As an example, the MYJCE provider defines the alias 3DES for the cipher algorithm whose standard name is DESede by setting a property named Alg.Alias.Cipher.3DES to have the value DESede via the following:

```
put("Alg.Alias.Cipher.3DES", "DESede");
```

Similarly, the following line enables users to specify TripleDES in place of 3DES:

```
put("Alg.Alias.Cipher.TripleDES", "DESede");
```

Currently, aliases defined by the MYJCE provider are available to all clients, no matter which provider clients request. For example, if another provider implements the DESede cipher algorithm, and the other provider does not provide an alias for it, the 3DES alias defined by MYJCE still can be used to refer to the other provider's DESede implementation, as follows:

```
Cipher ca = Cipher.getInstance("3DES", "OtherProvider")
```

Dependencies on other algorithms

Some algorithms require the use of other types of algorithms. For example, a Signature algorithm needs to use a message digest algorithm. To do this, you can do one of the following:

- Provide your own implementations for both.

- Let the implementation of one algorithm use an instance of the other type of algorithm provided by a specified provider. Using an instance of another type of algorithm is appropriate if the algorithm is provided by the Java 2 SDK or by the same provider. (Otherwise, you must be sure that all clients who use this provider also have the other provider installed.)

- Let the implementation of one algorithm use an instance of the other type of algorithm, as supplied by another (unspecified) provider. That is, you can request an algorithm by name, but without specifying any particular provider. This is only appropriate if you are sure that there is at least one implementation of the requested algorithm installed on each Java 2 SDK platform where your provider is used.

Default initializations

In case the client does not explicitly initialize a key pair generator or an algorithm parameter generator, each provider of such a service must supply (and document) a default initialization. For example, the SunJCE provider uses a default modulus key size of 1024 bits for the generation of Diffie-Hellman parameters.

Conclusion

Implementing services for your own JCA or JCE provider only requires a few steps. After implementing your services, such as new cipher classes, you can write a master class, then compile and package your classes. The resulting provider package is ready for use after you or the user modifies their Java security file or programmatically identifies your provider to the JVM.

Java cryptography Part 4: JCE export considerations

As you have learned in previous articles, JCE 1.2 from Sun provides a framework for encryption services into which implementations of any encryption algorithm from any (compliant) service provider can be plugged in. Currently, export control restrictions by the U.S. Commerce Department prohibit such a framework from being exported outside the U.S. or Canada, unless appropriate mechanisms have been implemented in the framework that would allow the framework to control the type of encryption algorithms and their cryptographic strength available to applications.

This article describes a possible approach that may make the next version of JCE (JCE 1.2.1) exportable.

Design Principles for Export

JCE 1.2.1 should be based on the following design principles:

- JCE 1.2.1 should take advantage of the security model introduced in Java 2 Standard Edition (J2SE), Version 1.2, from Sun. In particular, privileges related to the use of cryptography should be expressed as permission classes whose definition will be bundled with the JCE 1.2.1 framework.

- JCE 1.2.1 and NOT its cryptographic service providers (CSPs) should enforce restrictions regarding the cryptographic algorithms and key sizes available to applets/applications in different jurisdiction contexts.

- JCE 1.2.1 should be based on the existing JCE 1.2 and enhance it in order to become exportable. Backwards compatibility with JCE 1.2 should be maintained at the application level, i.e., applications written to JCE 1.2 will continue to work with JCE 1.2.1. However, JCE 1.2 compliant CSPs should be digitally signed in order to work with JCE 1.2.1. Existing applications should be treated as default applications, meaning the default jurisdiction policy file should determine the maximum allowable key size they can use.

- JCE 1.2.1 should be compatible with Sun's existing J2SE release and future versions of it. None of the new export features should require any new APIs or changes to existing APIs in J2SE.

- Applications that do not require any crypto stronger than the default strength (as defined by the applicable jurisdiction policy files) should not require any modifications (e.g., digital signing) by their vendor.

- CSPs should be written (and packaged) only once, implementing crypto of maximum strength. It is up to the JCE 1.2.1 framework and policy files to determine the maximum allowable strength for a given application in a given jurisdiction context.

- JCE 1.2.1 should be an exportable framework that can be shipped separately from its CSPs.

JCE 1.2.1 should have the same architecture and program flow as JCE 1.2. However, it should be enhanced in such a way that it can determine and restrict allowable key size for a given applet/application. The specific enhancements will be discussed in the following sections.

Mutual Authentication

In order to prevent unauthorized CSPs from plugging into JCE 1.2.1, and assure authorized providers of the integrity and authenticity of the JCE 1.2.1 version that they plug into, JCE 1.2.1 and its CSPs should engage in mutual authentication: Only CSPs that have authenticated the JCE 1.2.1 framework, and who in turn have been authenticated by JCE 1.2.1, should become usable in the JCE environment.

The JCE 1.2.1 framework should be digitally signed. An approved signer should digitally sign CSPs that provide implementations for JCE services. The javax.crypto.JceSecurity class, which is responsible for instantiating the JCE-related implementation classes of CSPs, should be used to authenticate a CSP. JCE 1.2.1 and its CSPs may be signed by different organizations, as long as their respective certificate chains can be traced back to a root certificate trusted by JCE 1.2.1 or its CSPs, respectively.

Since CSPs should continue to be registered through the java.security.Security class in the (core) J2SE, the mutual authentication between JCE 1.2.1 and its CSPs should not take place when the CSPs are registered, but later, when JCE 1.2.1 tries to instantiate a CSP's implementation of a JCE crypto service. That way, CSPs with implementations of cryptographic services defined in J2SE and JCE should be usable in the J2SE environment without having to engage in mutual authentication. Only those crypto services related to the JCE should have to engage in mutual authentication with the JCE 1.2.1

framework, and these services should become usable (in the JCE environment) only after such authentication has taken place.

How JCE authenticates a CSP

When instantiating a CSP's implementation (class) of a JCE service, JCE 1.2.1 should determine the CSP's codebase (JAR file) and verify its signature, using the digital signature mechanism and implementations provided by the Java Runtime Environment, which will include signature algorithms. JCE 1.2.1 should require that all Java class files in a CSP's JAR file be signed. This is to prevent a CSP (or one of its users) from inserting or replacing (unsigned) *helper* classes after the CSP has been signed. Furthermore, the same person or organization should sign all class files in the JAR.

How a CSP authenticates JCE

Every implementation class of a JCE-defined service in a CSP JAR file should authenticate the JCE 1.2.1 framework in its constructor, by determining the codebase of the JCE 1.2.1 JAR file and verifying its digital signature. This will help ensure that JCE 1.2.1 will be able to instantiate and use a CSP's implementation only after having been successfully authenticated by that CSP.

Implementation Rules for compliant CSPs

All Service Provider Interface (SPI) implementation classes in a CSP package should be declared public and have a public constructor in order for the JCE to be able to instantiate them.

For those classes to become unusable if instantiated by an application directly, bypassing the JCE, compliant CSPs should implement the following rules that should be checked as part of their compliance review process:

- All SPI implementation classes in a CSP package should be declared final (so that they cannot be subclassed), and their (SPI) implementation methods should be declared protected.

- All crypto-related helper classes in a CSP package should have package-private scope, so that they cannot be accessed from outside the CSP package.

Also, SPI implementation classes should authenticate the JCE 1.2.1 framework in their constructor.

A signer whose certificate chain can be traced back to a root certificate trusted by the JCE 1.2.1 framework should sign a JCE 1.2.1 compliant CSP.

JCE 1.2.1 Permission Model

JCE 1.2.1 should use two pairs of jurisdiction policy files: one for export outside the U.S. (manufacturing jurisdiction) and the other one applicable to the destination country where the JCE will be used (import or country-specific jurisdiction).

Each pair should contain two types of jurisdiction policy files: one for default, and the other one where the maximum key length is different from the default. Both the manufacturing and import jurisdiction policy files for default applications should be mandatory for enabling JCE 1.2.1, i.e., JCE 1.2.1 should not be usable without it.

JCE 1.2.1 should determine and enforce the weaker of the keysizes specified in the manufacturing and import jurisdiction policy files.

Each pair of jurisdiction policy files should be provided as a signed JAR file, which should be signed by the same entity (organization) that signed the JCE 1.2.1 framework JAR file, and should be provided in the same location where the JCE 1.2.1 framework JAR is stored.

JCE 1.2.1 should introduce a new permission class named javax.crypto.CryptoPermission (a subclass of java.security.Permission), which will reflect the ability of an application/applet to use certain algorithms with certain key sizes in certain environments. This should allow JCE 1.2.1 to represent its jurisdiction policy files as J2SE-style policy files with corresponding permission statements.

JCE 1.2.1 Exemption Mechanism

JCE 1.2.1 should define an exemption mechanism service module that could be used to implement key recovery, key weakening, or key escrow.

Applets and applications that require export or import restrictions should bundle with their JAR file a collection of javax.crypto.CryptoPermission objects that encapsulate the appropriate crypto permissions for using strong crypto (that was granted for a particular country). For applications/applets require the use of an exemption mechanism (such as key recovery), the crypto permissions should include the name of the exemption mechanism to be enforced.

The collection of crypto permissions should be signed by the same organization that signed the entire application JAR file, and should be granted only to the classes contained in the same JAR file.

If an applet/application requires key recover, key escrow or key weakening, JCE 1.2.1 should instantiate the required exemption mechanism implementation and pass it to the constructor of the API class (e.g., javax.crypto.Cipher) whose getInstance() factory method was called by the applet/application. That means that the API object returned to the applet/application should encapsulate an exemption mechanism API object whose restrictions it will enforce.

JCE 1.2.1 Enhancements to API Object Instantiation

Applications create an instance of a cryptographic service by calling that service's getInstance() factory method and specifying the name of the requested algorithm and optionally the name of the CSP from which the algorithm implementation is requested.

For example, in order to use the "Blowfish" implementation of a CSP named CryptoServices, Inc., an applet/application would make the following call:

```
Cipher c = Cipher.getInstance("Blowfish", "CryptoServices, Inc.");
```

All getInstance() methods of JCE-defined crypto services are routed through the javax.crypto.JceSecurity class, which is responsible for instantiating the implementation class of the requested algorithm (from the requested CSP) and making sure that it is an instance of the appropriate SPI class (e.g., an instance of javax.crypto.CipherSpi in the above example). The implementation object is then returned to the caller (i.e., the getInstance() method), which encapsulates it into an instance of javax.crypto.Cipher and returns that to the applet/application.

Any method calls on the new javax.crypto.Cipher object that was returned are no longer routed through JceSecurity, but invoke the corresponding SPI methods of the encapsulated javax.crypto.CipherSpi implementation object directly. That means that when an application calls Cipher.getInstance(), JCE 1.2.1 determines the maximum allowable key size and exemption mechanism (if applicable) and pass that information to the constructor of the API (wrapper) class, so that it can then enforce those restrictions when mapping API calls onto the corresponding SPI methods of the encapsulated SPI object.

Two additional parameters should be added: em (of type ExemptionMechanism) and maxKeySize (of type int) to the constructor of every affected API class in JCE 1.2.1. Those constructors get invoked by the (static) getInstance() factory method of their respective classes. In JCE 1.2, the constructors take an SPI implementation instance and CSP information as parameters. The new em and maxKeySize constructor arguments should be saved as private fields in the resulting API instance. Get methods in the affected JCE 1.2.1 API classes should be defined, so that an applet/application can retrieve the values of those fields and possibly call the methods on the ExemptionMechanism instance directly, if needed.

An API class (e.g., javax.crypto.Cipher) should compare the value of its maxKeySize field with the size of the Key object with which it gets initialized (during javax.crypto.Cipher.init()), making sure the actual key size is less than or equal to the maximum allowable key size, before passing the Key object down to the corresponding engineInit() method of the encapsulated SPI implementation instance.

JCE 1.2.1 Security Manager

J2SE defines a special permission class named java.security.AllPermission, which implies every other single permission. If an application was granted this type of permission, it could use cryptographic algorithms and keys of any strength, because AllPermission would also imply any of the crypto-related permissions in JCE 1.2.1. JCE 1.2.1 should prevent that by instantiating its own security manager (a subclass of java.lang.SecurityManager), which should also be responsible for determining the maximum allowable key size for a given algorithm for a given applet/application.

Note that JCE 1.2.1 instantiates its own security manager and not install it. Therefore, the JCE 1.2.1 security manager should not interfere with a security manager already installed (e.g., the applet security manager).

The JCE 1.2.1 security manager determines the allowable key size for a given applet/application by taking into account the installed jurisdiction policy files (after having verified their digital signature) and any crypto permissions (of type javax.crypto.CryptoPermission) that the applet/application may have bundled with its JAR file.

The JCE 1.2.1 security manager determines if the applet/application was granted any crypto permissions in its JAR file.

Choosing the right cryptography for your e-business application

There comes a time in the development of your network or application program when you need to introduce security, whether to authenticate senders or encrypt mail or transactions for recipients. Many cryptographic algorithms have been vetted and enumerated in standards, so how do you choose the best ones for you and your application? This article discusses the popular cryptographic algorithms that are in widespread use today and suggests which ones might be best suited to your network or application as part of your Public Key Infrastructure (PKI) solution. It also discusses the availability of the PKI algorithms in the Java environment.

Public Key algorithms

Other articles in this book introduced the technologies behind public and private keys and their importance to authentication and encryption. After creating their public and private key pair, users can wrap a certificate around their public key and place it on an external certificate directory for all to access. Users would keep their private key hidden. A message or transaction encrypted with a public key can be decrypted with a private key, or vice versa.

In PKI, public and private keys provide the foundation for authenticated messages. Byte information can be hashed and signed with a private key to create a digital signature of the message. Using a tenet of the public key algorithms, recipients of a signed message can run the contents and signature of the message along with the signer's public key through a verification algorithm that matches the signing algorithm. If the verification algorithm returns true, the recipient knows the message came from the signer.

The two most popular public-key algorithms are RSA, named after its inventors using the first letter of their last names, and the Digital Signature Algorithm (DSA). Both algorithms have their advantages. Web browsers popularized the use of RSA and the algorithm remains in widespread use today. The National Institute of Standards and Technology (NIST) created DSA, which became a general, royalty-free algorithm for signing messages.

With RSA, users can create key sizes that generally range from 512 to 2048 bits, but they can go higher. A larger key size provides greater security against attackers, but it also slows down the algorithm. For numerous transactions over a long period of time, this performance degradation can become significant. Therein emanates one of the general rules of security: The greater the level of security, the slower the performance. RSA keys also are versatile enough to be used for encryption, as defined in PKCS #1.

With DSA public and private keys, you can sign and verify messages, but you cannot use the keys for general encryption and decryption. DSA key sizes can range from 512 to 1024 bits.

Java applications can take advantage of DSA and RSA. The Java Cryptography Architecture (JCA) included in every Java Runtime Environment (JRE) contains support for DSA public and private keys. Java Cryptography Extension (JCE) providers can include support for RSA. Users should obtain a JCE provider implementation separately from the JRE, since the JCE also includes support for encryption, which is subject to export controls.

If a Java application only supports DSA keys, users or administrators do not need to modify their configuration. In this case, they are using the default DSA implementation provided by the Java platform. If developers choose to support RSA keys or if the user has the ability to specify either type of key, all users need to do is configure their Java security file to locate the JCE provider that includes support for the DSA or RSA algorithms.

Selecting a key size

RSA public and private keys offer a greater key size range than DSA. In general, some form of cryptography is better than none and stronger cryptography is preferable to weak cryptography. This strategy would suggest that the strongest key size always be used, however, developers must weigh the tradeoffs between making their products more secure and hampering their performance. Let's examine the   popular public and private key sizes of 512, 1024, and 2048. Note that DSA has a key size limit of 1024 bits.

Key sizes of 512 bits are generally recognized to be unsecure because they can be broken relatively quickly. In years past, a 512 key size was secure, but due to the increase in computing power, messages encrypted with keys of 512 bits can be broken after a short period of time. If you have to choose between no encryption and encryption with a 512 key size, the 512 key will impede the attacker to some extent. However, this choice should not give you – as a developer or user – a false sense of security.

Key sizes of 1024 bits are the most popular ones in use for commercial transactions. They are a common staple in e-business today, as many sites will establish secret key agreement sessions, such as via the Secure Sockets Layer (SSL) that are based upon a 1024-bit key. Key sizes of 768 have been promoted for personal certificates, but the trend is towards using 1024-bit keys for personal certificates as well.

Key sizes of 2048 bits are less common and typically used for transactions that require stronger security. As mentioned earlier, the stronger the security, the greater the impact on performance. Unless you have a compelling need for the strongest generally available security – and you would for the most sensitive data – many applications can implement a comfortable level of security with 1024-bit keys.

Signature algorithms

With the public and private key algorithm and key size decided, you'll need to pick a signature algorithm, both for your certificate and for signed messages that you originate. The signature algorithm is made up of two parts, the message digest and the public key algorithm. The type of your private key governs the latter. You have some flexibility in specifying your message digest, depending on your public key algorithm.

A message digest algorithm takes any length of data and creates a hash of the data that is of a short, defined length, such as 16 or 20 bytes. Message digest algorithms are designed so that one cannot reverse engineer the digest to get the original data. Message digests are used within the signature process, since it is faster and more efficient for the signature algorithm to encrypt a small digest than a large number of bytes.

For RSA, you can choose from a number of message digest algorithms: Message Digest 2 (MD2), MD5, and Secure Hash Algorithm-1 (SHA-1). MD2 is an older algorithm that is still supported by most applications. MD5 is a popular, newer version. At one time MD4 existed, but it was pulled after security problems were discovered. SHA-1 is a successor to SHA and is another widely used message digest algorithm. Since SHA was withdrawn, SHA typically implies SHA-1. SHA-1 is considered more secure since it produces a larger digest, 20 bytes, in comparison to the 16-byte digest created by MD2 and MD5. If you chose MD5 or SHA1 as your message digest algorithm, your signature algorithm would be MD5withRSA or SHA1withRSA.

For DSA, you can only select one message digest algorithm, SHA-1. This gives you a signature algorithm of SHA1withDSA.

Secret key algorithms

To complete your selection of algorithms for general PKI applications, you need to choose a secret key or encryption algorithm. Secret key algorithms are much faster than public key algorithms, but by themselves, they lack the ability to authenticate the sender or recipient of the message. That is why secret keys and public keys are used together to send secret messages. The initial steps of authentication and secret key exchange are performed using public key technology. Afterwards, the remainder of the encrypted data exchange is done under the much-faster secret key.

As defined in PKCS #7, the application that creates the EnvelopedData object generates a secret key, encrypts the message with the secret key, and encrypts the secret key with the public key of the recipient. The receiver of the EnvelopedData object decrypts the secret key with the private key that corresponded to the public key. With the secret key in hand, the recipient can decrypt the ciphered text. This process ensures that the application does not send the secret key in the clear with the message and that only the intended recipients can decrypt the message.

Three secret key algorithms are in widespread use today: RC2, Data Encryption Standard (DES), and TripleDES (3DES). (Many others exist as well.) RC2 came into being as an alternative to DES since applications implementing RC2 with a 40-bit key had a greater opportunity to be approved for export. Nowadays, key sizes of 40-bits are considered weak encryption, and as we will see, larger key sizes are needed.

DES has been in widespread use and was adopted by the U.S. Government for many years, but with its 56-bit key, it has grown vulnerable with the increase of computing power available. The NIST recognized this and is working toward the creation of a new standard for encryption, the Advanced Encryption Standard (AES). While the final algorithm for AES is being selected, the NIST recommends that applications switch to TripleDES with its 168-bit key size. As the name suggests, TripleDES is a variation of DES that uses the same or different 56-bit keys three times to encrypt or decrypt the data.

Secret key algorithms, like TripleDES, require only one key to encrypt or decrypt data. As mentioned earlier, RSA public and private keys can be used alone to encrypt text. The RSA public key can encrypt data and the corresponding private key can decrypt it, or vice versa. Encryption algorithms that use only one key, such as secret key, are known as symmetric algorithms. Encryption algorithms that use a key pair, such as a public and private key, are known as asymmetric algorithms.

Since export laws restrict encryption algorithms, their implementation in Java security is available within a JCE provider, which is not part of the generally distributed JRE. The good news is that once users or developers acquire one or more JCE providers, they can have all the algorithms that they need to create a robust and secure PKI application.

An example

Take the example where Benjamin, a developer for Antietam Software, wants to implement security for his Internet application. He first selects RSA as his public and private key algorithm since he may want to use the keys later for encryption or decryption. Since he is creating a standard e-business application, he chooses a 1024-bit key size. He generates his key pair and sends his public key to a Certificate Authority (CA), requesting that the CA create a certificate that will be associated with his application. Ben receives the certificate from the CA and imbeds it into his application.

When the application uses the certificate to sign a message or transaction that it sends, Ben selects SHA1withRSA as the signing algorithm. SHA1 is the latest recommended message digest algorithm and RSA is Ben's the public key algorithm selection. For encryption, Ben selects TripleDES since that is also the latest standard secret key algorithm.

Conclusion

To implement a robust and secure PKI application, you need to select from the set the standard cryptographic algorithms, since they have been vetted for completeness and security. This article introduces many of the popular ones from which to choose. With knowledge of the various, standard algorithms and their security and performance impacts, you can select the right ones for your e-business application.

Public Key Technologies

In this section, we introduce the *key* technology to successful e-business deployments – public keys. Public and private key pairs breached the limitations of prior security solutions and enabled an entire realm of applications. Almost all e-business sites utilize public keys to some extent. Join us as we begin with an introduction to what public keys offer and their manifestation in certificates. We continue with a description of the signing process and give you tips on how to detect invalid messages, an essential ability to building a secure web of trust.

- Why public keys?

- On the trail of certificates in Java security

- Signing and verifying with certificates in Java security

- When cryptographic messages go bad

- Certificate paths – Weaving a web of trust

- Unshackling key management in Java security

Why public keys?

Public key technologies have become the staple of successful e-business applications, but why? What makes their use and exploitation essential? This article delves into the problems and requirements that public key technologies successfully address and serves as an introduction to the other articles in this section.

Business Requirements

To serve nonsensitive information to customers over the Internet, such as general information, organizations and individuals do not need high levels of security, other than the server-side protection required to keep their Web sites running and fend off malicious attacks. To conduct business over the unsecured Internet realm, business should bring their Web sites to the next level to provide trust and confidentiality, not only for themselves, but also for the customers they wish to attract.

•   The need for e-business security can be distilled into the following high-level requirements:

•   Need to send secure and identifiable transactions over an unsecured network. Transactions can range from binary exchanges over a socket to asynchronous messages.

Need to publicize information about oneself for business transactions.

Scenarios

Examine the high-level requirements in the following e-business scenarios:

(1)   An on-line retailer needs a way for customers to send personal information in private as part of a transaction. This private information could include the customer's address and credit card number. Without confidentiality for this information, the retailer will not be able to convince customers to purchase products from the site. In this example as part of a transaction of buying products from an e-business retailer, customers must know that malevolent third parties cannot intercept their credit card information. Retailers need the credit card number to complete the transaction, and they also need the ability to allow for purchases by credit card since they are much

more efficient and customers are less likely to follow through on purchases by check or other slower methods for non-critical purchases.

(2)   In a business-to-business (B2B) transaction, employees of different companies need to send sensitive messages to each other. They could use regular e-mail programs to send this information in message over the Internet, but they would require security beyond that provided by regular Multipurpose Internet Mail Extension (MIME) messages. In this example, Ben needs to send confidential bidding information to Sarah, but Ben only wants Sarah to see the information. Sarah wants to know that Ben was the one who sent the message and that no one altered the message before it got to her.

(3)   For companies or individuals to contact other business or entities, they must be able to acquire information about the recipients of the communication in a standard and verifiable manner. In this example, Patrick needs to publicize information about himself, so that others can send secure messages to him, but he does not want to advertise any private information about himself. Recipients of Patrick's information must be able to verify that this data is correct.

Essential Requirements

To meet the problem requirements as introduced in these scenarios, any technological solution must be able to provide:

- Confidentiality—Protect the contents of the transaction from unintended recipients.

- Authentication—Guarantee that the transaction originated from the sender.

- Integrity—Ensure that the transaction was not modified in transit.

- Publication—Provide trusted management of the public information used.

Previous Solutions

Previous solutions to the problem included the following:

- Closed Systems—By themselves or in a network, workstations in a guarded area and not connected to the public Internet provide highly controlled security. While there is strength in isolation, such solutions cannot play on the public and heterogeneous Internet and are thus locked out of expanding their customer or user base.

- Secret keys—Ciphers that employ a single secret key have many advantages. They can encrypt and decrypt bulk data quickly and their algorithms have been thoroughly examined and tested. However, secret keys only solve the confidentiality requirement, and this restricts their advantages. Remaining unanswered are how the keys should be shared between the sender and receiver and how does the receiver know that encrypted information came from the sender? More importantly, what happens when a secret key is lost? A misplaced or stolen key compromises all past and future transactions encrypted by the lost key.

Motivation for Public Key Technologies

Given the shortcomings of previous solutions, successful Internet companies quickly gravitated to the technology and promise of public key solutions. Public Key algorithms generate a unique public and private key and the use of these keys in various standards address the vast requirements of our e-business scenarios.

- Confidentiality—A public key can encrypt information that only the corresponding private key can decrypt or vice versa. The associated public key can only decrypt data encrypted by a private key.

- Authentication—A recipient of a message with a certificate that contains the sender's public key can trace the sender's certificate to a trusted authority that can verify the identity of the sender.

- Integrity—Recipients of a message signed by the sender's private key can use the sender's public key to verify that the message did not change in transit.

- Publication—When an application generates a public and private key pair for a business or individual, the private key is meant to be kept hidden by the possessing entity, but the public key can be advertised to anyone. Public keys can be published in a standard and trusted fashion as certificates, using such standards as X.509.

Public key technologies use standards that promote interoperability between different vendors. These standards are public and that have been vetted for completeness and security, which allowed possible flaws in the standards to be quickly exposed and corrected. While the algorithms are public, keys generated by the algorithms are not. These keys are unique to the random parameters passed in by the caller. Public key algorithms include RSA and DSA.

Note that public key technologies do not currently cover authorization requirements, the set of rules as to whether or not a user should have access to a set of data. Authorization remains a requirement specific to each business scenario. For example, authenticated employees of Antietam Software should be able to read general bulletins about the company on an Intranet site, but they should not be able to access sensitive information about other employees, such as software developer Benjamin, through the same portal. The authorization policies instituted by the administrator and corporation could govern that only the employee and his or her immediate manager can view their personnel records.

Public key technologies are also referred to as the Public Key Infrastructure X.509 (PKIX). The core of PKIX addresses key management, but PKIX also extends to the use of public keys to fulfill the requirements. For more in-depth information about public keys and their exploitation, continue your journey with the other articles in this section.

On the trail of certificates in Java security

As the e-business market expands, so too does the role and importance of certificates. This article provides an overview of certificates and traces their use in Java 2 security.

Certificates and public keys

A certificate represents the public identity of a person or entity. At the heart of a certificate is the person's public key. The public key architecture relies upon two keys for every person—a private and a public key. The public key can be freely distributed to the outside world, but the person who owns the key keeps the private key in confidence. The public key is used in verifying that data signed with the private key originated from the person who is associated with the public key. Anything, such as a file, encrypted with a private key can be decrypted by the private key's associated public key and vice versa.

Since the public key consists of a collection of bits, it cannot be identified by itself. Attaching a text string or distinguished name to the public key helps to identify the owner of the keys, but the association by itself still doesn't lend validity to the public key, since anyone could have attached the name to the public key. A trusted third party or issuer of the certificate needs to verify that the public key belongs to the person, and the identification of the issuer also is included as part of the certificate. Certificates are generally issued by a Certificate Authority (CA) and the CA bundles and signs the entire set of information to create a certificate for the person.

Take the example where Benjamin wants to send Patrick a file signed with Ben's private key. How does Patrick know that Ben actually sent the file? Benjamin first passes the file through an algorithm to produce a message digest. The message digest is a hash key that represents the file. The message digest is important because the recipient of the file can run the file through the same message digest algorithm to generate a hash key. If the message digest sent with the file matches the generated message digest, the recipient can trust that no one has tampered with the file's contents.

Next, Benjamin encrypts the message digest with his private key. The encrypted message digest is known as the signature of the file. With the file digitally signed, Ben can distribute it to Patrick. When Patrick receives the file and its signature, he already has Ben's public key that he acquired from some means. For example, Ben could have sent him the public key earlier through a secure channel, Ben's public key could be wrapped in a certificate that was sent with the file, or Patrick could look up Ben's certificate in an LDAP database.

However he acquired it, Patrick can use Ben's public key to decrypt the signature. Patrick also runs the file through the message digest algorithm. If the decrypted signature and generated message digest match, Patrick can rest assured that the file came from Benjamin and not his nemesis, PoMiester. The comparison also validates that the file contents have not been changed.

In the Java world, signed classes, their message digests and the signing certificate are generally packaged together in a Java Archive (JAR) file. The process of verifying signatures and files is generally performed under the covers by the Web browser or Java program, so that the user does not need to manually execute the steps, unless desired. For example, should the user receive a signed JAR file, the user can utilize the Java jarsigner tool, discussed later in more detail, to verify that the file belongs to the signer and that the contents have not changed.

X.509 certificates

In the Java realm, and indeed across the e-business world, the most common format for certificates is X.509. The X.509 certificate contains the following certificate elements:

1. Version number. Most X.509 certificates in use today are at version 1. CAs also issue version 3 certificates, which are the most recent. Certificates at the version 3 level contain extensions to indicate such attributes as whether or not the certificate can be used to sign objects or remain only as identification.

2. Subject DN. The name of the person or entity to whom the certificate belongs adheres to the X.500 standard for a Distinguished Name (DN). For example, the following could be Benjamin's DN:

    CN=Benjamin, OU=Antietam Software, O=IBM, ST=TX, C=US

3. Public key and its format. This key can be used by recipients of signed files to verify that the document came from the person or entity identified by the Subject DN. The format indicates the encryption algorithm used, as well as the message digest algorithm.

4. Issuer DN. The name of the entity, typically a CA, who issued the certificate for the subject DN.

5. Serial number. This identification value is unique for the Issuer DN. CAs use serial numbers when creating Certificate Revocation Lists (CRLs).

6.   Validity range. The certificate is valid between the specified start and end dates and times, as established by the CA. Processes that generate and use certificates between themselves typically use short validation times. Persons who use a certificate to identify their work generally have longer validation times.

7.   Signature. The CA bundles all of the above information and other attributes and creates an encrypted message digest. The recipient of the certificate can verify the signature to ensure that the certificate has not been compromised.

Message digests are created with a specific algorithm. The most common algorithms are RSA and DSA. By default, the Java Runtime Environment (JRE) provides support for DSA and uses this algorithm for creating key pairs. When creating self-signed certificates, Java security currently defaults to using the SHA1with DSA signature algorithm and sets the validity range to 90 days. Many certificates, such as those used to sign Netscape JAR files, use the RSA algorithm. The JRE can support the RSA algorithm if the user or the Java program registers an RSA service provider. Web browsers, such as Netscape, also support RSA signed certificates.

The recipient of a certificate may be interested in following the chain of certificates leading up to the root CA certificate. Following the certificate chain ensures that the certificate was issued from the specified Issuer DN and provides another way of checking that the certificate is valid. Most Web browsers are shipped with trusted root CA certificates to aid in verifying the certificate chain. Within the Java environment, trusted certificates for Java programs that are run outside of the Web browser are stored in the cacerts file, typically located in $(java.home)\lib\security.

Developers typically create self-signed certificates that are used as part of testing. As part of the build or test environment, developers easily can generate self-signed certificates since they do not require a CA or a monetary fee for their creation. Once product development is further along, developers can obtain a certificate from a trusted CA—typically one of the more popular ones whose public certificates are well known. Self-signed certificates generally are not used in a production environment since recipients cannot follow the certificate chain to a trusted CA.

Certificate tools

The Java 2 Standard Development Kit (SDK) provides the keytool program to help developers and users manage keystores and certificates. Public and private keys, as well as certificates, are stored in a keystore. Java security uses its own format for the default keystore shipped with the JRE.

The Java 2 SDK also provides the jarsigner program to help sign JAR files or verify the signatures on signed JAR files. The jarsigner tool works by verifying that the files in the JAR file were signed with the certificate stored with the JAR file and that the certificate exists in the user's keystore. The Java 2 keytool and jarsigner programs replace the javakey program in JDK 1.1.

Developers and users can utilize keytool to create a Sun public and private key pair and a self-signed X509 version 1 certificate in the Java keystore, such as with the following command:

```
keytool -genkey -alias certAlias -keypass keyPwd -dname dnName
```

where certAlias is the alias name of the key pair and accompanying certificate and keyPwd is the private key password name. The value for dnName is the Subject DN, such as "cn=Common Name, o=IBM, c=US". The keystore location defaults to the .keystore file in the user's home directory, since it was not specified. The keytool program will prompt the user for the password that protects the certificate database.

Developers and users can check that the keytool created the certificate with the following command:

```
keytool -list
```

Once a self-signed certificate has been created, developers and users can utilize the jarsigner tool to sign a JAR file with their certificate.

Java 2 security

Java 2 security represents X.509 certificates with the X509Certificate abstract class. In the implementing class, assorted methods allow the caller to retrieve X.509 certificate attributes.

Each loaded class has a CodeSource associated with it. The CodeSource object consists of a codebase that is comprised of the URL from which the class was retrieved and the set of certificates that signed the class, if any. Additionally, Java security associates a CodeSource with a set of permissions.

Thus, objects can determine the permissions that they are granted by examining their ProtectionDomain. An object can determine its code source by first getting its class with the getClass() method and by calling the retrieving class' ProtectionDomain and inner CodeSource through follow up calls. For example, the following code retrieves the CodeSource for object myobject:

```
CodeSource cs =
    myobject.getClass().getProtectionDomain().getCodeSource();
```

Developers can retrieve the certificates that were used to sign the class by calling the getCertificates() method on the CodeSource object.

Note that the core classes do not have a ProtectionDomain and this also implies that they have been granted AllPermission.

When a class is loaded from a signed JAR file, the JRE will verify that the certificate in the JAR file signed the classes in the JAR file and that the certificate exists in the specified keystore. If not, the JRE treats the entire JAR file as unsigned and the classes in the JAR file lose any special permissions that may have been granted to the certificate and codebase combination. The JRE will create a ProtectionDomain, if one did not exist for the CodeSource that associates the CodeSource from which the JAR was loaded with the set of matching permissions from the Java Policy object. When started, the JRE creates the Java Policy object by loading and interpreting all the policy files specified in the java.security file.

Certificate example

The following program demonstrates how to view the attributes on a certificate with which a class was signed. The program takes a class name as input and retrieves the ProtectionDomain for the class. Within the ProtectionDomain lies the CodeSource object and the set of certificates for the class. The program displays a number of X.509 certificate attributes, including the Subject DN, Issuer DN and validity range.

Note that Java 2 security upgraded the old java.security.Certificate class to java.security.cert.Certificate. Since Java 2 security retains the old Certificate class for backwards compatibility, this program explicitly uses the java.security.cert package name. Alternatively, the program could have imported the specific classes the java.security and java.security.cert packages instead of importing all the classes in both packages.

ShowCert.java

```
package ibm.book;

import java.security.*;
import java.security.cert.*;

public class ShowCert {
    public static void main(String args[]) {
```

```
if (args.length == 0) {
   System.out.println(
      "Specify a class name for which to show certificates.");
      return;
}

String classname = args[0];
System.out.println("Showing certificates for "+ classname);
Class cl;

try {
   cl = Class.forName(classname);
} catch (Exception e) {
   System.out.println("Could not find " + classname);
   System.out.println("    Exception: " + e);
   return;
}

ProtectionDomain pd = cl.getProtectionDomain();
CodeSource cs = pd.getCodeSource();

java.security.cert.Certificate[] certs = cs.getCertificates();

if (certs == null) {
   System.out.println("Class " + classname
      + " was not signed with any certificates");
   return;
}
System.out.println("Class " + classname + " was signed by "
   + certs.length + " certificate(s).");

for (int i=0;i<certs.length;i++) {
   X509Certificate cert = (X509Certificate) certs[i];
   System.out.println("Certificate #"+i);
   System.out.println("\tVersion = " + cert.getVersion());
   System.out.println("\tSubjectDN = " + cert.getSubjectDN());
   System.out.println("\tKey algorithm = " + cert.getSigAlgName());
   System.out.println("\tIssuerDN = " + cert.getIssuerDN());
   System.out.println("\tSerial Number = " + cert.getSerialNumber());
   System.out.println("\tValidity between " + cert.getNotBefore()
      + " and " + cert.getNotAfter());

   try {
      cert.checkValidity();
```

```
        System.out.println("\tCertificate is valid.");
    } catch (Exception e) {
        System.out.println("\tCertificate is not valid.");
        System.out.println("\tException: " + e);
    }
  }
}
}
```

To build the program, package the class in a JAR file and sign it with your certificate, such as with the following commands:

```
jar cvf cert.jar <dir where ShowCert.class is located>
jarsigner -storepass jsStorePass -keypass jsKeyPass
       -signedjar scert.jar cert.jar BenAlias
```

The jsStorePass and jsKeyPass values reflect the keystore and private key passwords respectively. The jarsigner tool will take the cert.jar file and sign it with the certificate alias name BenAlias to create the signed JAR file scert.jar. This example signs the JAR file with only one certificate, but the JAR file can be signed with multiple certificates. With the scert.jar file in the CLASSPATH, run the program to display the certificate that signed the ShowCert class with the following command:

```
java ibm.book.ShowCert ibm.book.Showcert
```

For the default Policy File implementation, use the signed by value for a permission grant entry to assign permissions to classes that are signed by a specific certificate. Remember to include the location of your keystore file so Java security can correlate the certificate alias name to an entry in the keystore file. For example, to give Benjamin, a developer with Antietam Software, read access to all files on your C: drive, include the following in your specified java.policy file:

```
keystore ".keystore", "jks";
grant signedBy "BenAlias"{
    permission java.io.FilePermission "c:\\-", "read";
};
```

Conclusion

Certificates play a key role in security, and X.509 certificates are the most common in e-business. Because users can verify the contents of files and trace a certificate back to a trusted CA, the use of certificates helps build a web of trust for users. Java 2 security integrates certificates into its security model, especially within its security objects, such as CodeSource and ProtectionDomain. Administrators and users can assign permissions to classes that have been signed with a specific certificate.

Signing and verifying with certificates in Java security

In the "On the Trail of Certificates in Java security" article, we discussed certificates, their representation in Java security, and their importance in e-business. This article delves deeper into the use of certificates in Java security, particularly their use in signing data and verifying signatures. A later example demonstrates how to create a signature for a message and verify the authenticity of the signature using classes that are part of the Java Runtime Environment (JRE).

Overview of the signing process

Certificates represent the public identity of a user or entity as granted by a certificate authority. Certificates also exploit the public key architecture. In this model, a selected algorithm will generate a public and private key pair. The key pair holds a special relationship. Only the accompanying public key can decrypt data that has been encrypted by a private key. The reverse relationship also is true. Only the associated private key can decrypt data encrypted by a public key. After a key pair is generated for a user, the public key is stored within the user's public certificate and the private key is squirreled away and kept hidden by the user. These public and private key pairs play a pivotal role in signing data and verifying signatures.

Signing raw data or data representations of objects involves two steps. First, the signing process produces a message digest of the data. Next, the signing process encrypts the digest with the private key to create a signature of the data. When the sender transmits data with its generated signature to another user, the recipient can verify the signature with the public key that is associated with the private key used in signing. Commonly signed data objects include applet JAR files and e-mail messages.

Figure 5 shows the steps of the signing process in more detail.

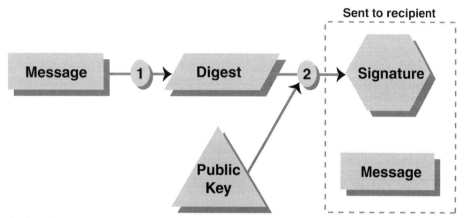

1. Apply message digest algorithm
2. Apply signature creation algorithm

Figure 5: Message signing process

Message digest

A generated message digest represents a unique hash code for the digested data. Algorithms that create message digests endeavor to ensure that the generated digest is unique, so that even the slightest change to the original data causes the new digest to be different from the old. The algorithms also ensure the digest itself cannot be used as part of a reverse engineering process to discover the original data.

Popular message digest algorithms include SHA-1 and MD5, although the use of MD5 has waned in favor of the stronger SHA-1 algorithm. The MD2 and MD4 algorithms are outdated and should not be used, due to their short key length or vulnerability.

Message digests help recipients verify the integrity of the digested data. As useful as message digests are, they cannot be used for authentication. If a user receives data and its accompanying digest, the user can use the same message digest algorithm on the data to compute the digest and compare the computed digest against the received digest. If they match, users can be sure that the data has not changed. However, users cannot be certain that the sender of the data and digest is bona fide. The transformation of the digest to a signature value allows the recipient to authenticate the source of the data.

Generating signatures

To add authentication to the signature process, the sender must put the digest through another step where the digest is encrypted with the sender's private key. The result of the encryption is a signature, an encrypted digest. For the sender to allow the recipient to authenticate the received data, the sender would need to send the data to the recipient with the data's signature. Note that the digest was encrypted and not the message itself.

Popular signature algorithms include DSA, which is the default supplied with Java security, and RSA, which is supported by various entities, such as Netscape Web browsers. The signature algorithm attribute on a certificate typically is identified with the combination of the message digest and encryption algorithms. For example, "SHA1withRSA" indicates that the signature for the accompanying data was generated by creating a message digest of the data with the SHA1 algorithm and encrypting the digest with the RSA algorithm.

Verifying signatures

To verify a signature, the recipient needs the data, its signature and the certificate of the sender. Since the sender transmitted it, the recipient already has the data and its signature. The recipient can retrieve the sender's certificate as part of an accessible certificate database or LDAP directory, for example, if it wasn't sent with the message. With only these three objects, the recipient can verify the integrity of the data as well as the authenticity of the sender.

Figure 6 shows the steps of the verification process in more detail.

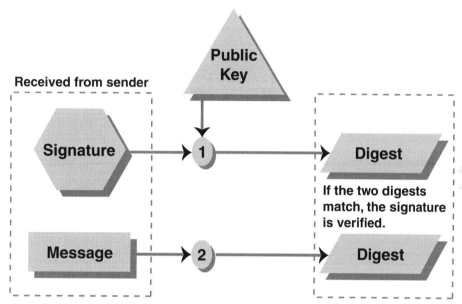

1. **Apply signature verification algorithm**
2. **Apply message digest algorithm**

Figure 6: Message verification process

The verification process begins by extracting the signature algorithm and public key from the sender's certificate. The signature algorithm tells the verification process which message digest and encryption algorithm was used in the signing process.

The verification process uses the encryption algorithm and the sender's public key to decrypt the signature. Next, the verification process uses the message digest algorithm to compute an independent message digest of the data. Lastly, the process compares the independently computed digest with the decrypted signature. If the two are the same, verification succeeds and the recipient can sleep well knowing the data was authenticated and its integrity validated. If the two values differ, the recipient is altered that something is wrong.

Java classes

The Java 2 JRE contains a framework for signing and verification and includes some implementations of public domain cryptography algorithms sufficient to allow developers to sign and verify data. The basic security classes that include support for message digests and signatures are part of the Java Cryptographic Architecture (JCA). However, the JRE does not contain classes to encrypt or decrypt data. Ciphers, key exchange algorithms and their accompanying classes are part of the Java Cryptographic Environment (JCE) package. The JCE is restricted for export and thus is packaged separately. The JCE also plugs into the JCA, and the JCA is subject to U.S. export regulations so that other companies can provide additional packages that support other security classes, such as RSA signatures.

Generating a signature includes encryption, but since the encryption is restricted to the message digest of an object or data, the encryption can be part of the signature process that is included with the JRE. With the JRE classes, developers cannot encrypt or decrypt arbitrary data.

An example

The following example illustrates how developers can sign data and verify signatures within Java security. For conciseness, both the signing and verification steps are performed in the same example program and not all the error checking has been included.

The signing and verification processes are typically broken into different modules or applications. The Public-Key Cryptography Standards (PKCS) #7 provides a standard in which data and its signature can be bundled into a SignedData object and transmitted to other heterogeneous applications. The Distinguished Encoding Rules (DER) encoded definition for SignedData includes the data, signature and identity of the sender. The recipient would need to look up the identity in a certificate database to retrieve the certificate that contains the sender's private key. The DER encoding of the SignedData object could be delivered to the recipient application via a socket or file, for example.

In the following example, Benjamin wants to send the following important message to Patrick: "Lee and McClellan are at Antietam." Ben is not concerned about encrypting the message but wants Patrick to know that the message originated from Ben and that no one modified the message in transit.

This example uses the default Java keystore that handles the DSA signature format for its certificates. The program loads the keystore and obtains Ben's certificate before extracting the public key, which is used in the verification process. In a separate step, the program also retrieves the private key, which would only be used in the signature process and only be known to Ben.

To generate a signature, the program utilizes an instance of the Signature object to create a message digest of the data and encrypt the digest. To get an instance of the Signature object within the JCA framework, the calling program must specifying the desired algorithm with the getInstance static method. Before the Signature instance can be used for signing, it must be initialized with the initSign method that takes Ben's private key as an argument. The program feeds the message into the Signature instance with the update method and retrieves the signature with the sign method.

The verification process is similar, in that the program first must get an instance of the Signature class, but to initialize it, the program instead calls the initVerify method with Ben's public key. The message is fed into the Signature instance as before, but now the program calls the verify method with the signature that accompanied Ben's message as input. The verify method returns true if the decrypted signature matches the computed digest.

Thus, if Patrick wanted to verify a message and signature that Ben sent, Patrick could call the verifySignature method in this example from his own module. If Patrick received a return of true from the method with the first digest, Patrick would know that it was his friend Ben who sent the message. If Patrick received false from the method, such as with the fake message, Patrick would know that the message did not come from Ben or that the message was changed in transit.

Note that if you specify the signature algorithm as DSA, the JCA will map the DSA alias to the fully expanded SHA1withDSA signature algorithm.

SignAndVerify.java

```
package ibm.book;

import java.io.*;
import java.security.*;
import java.security.cert.*;

public class SignAndVerify {

    String message = "Lee and McClellan are at Antietam.";
    String fakemessage =
      "Lee is at Richmond and McClellan is at Washington.";
    String keystoreFilename =
      "C:\\WINNT40\\Profiles\\Administrator\\.keystore";
    String certificateAlias = "benalias";
```

```java
String privateKeyName = "benalias";
String privateKeyPassword = "BenPwd";
String signatureAlgorithm = "SHA1withDSA";

X509Certificate x509cert;
PublicKey publicKey;
PrivateKey privateKey;

public static void main(String args[]) {
  SignAndVerify prog = new SignAndVerify();
  prog.run();
}

public void run() {
  try {
  System.out.println("Loading the keystore and retrieving keys.");
  // using the JavaSoft keystore
  KeyStore ks = KeyStore.getInstance("JKS");
  FileInputStream ksinputstream =
      new FileInputStream(keystoreFilename);
  ks.load(ksinputstream, null);

  x509cert = (X509Certificate) ks.getCertificate(certificateAlias);
  publicKey = x509cert.getPublicKey();
  privateKey = (PrivateKey) ks.getKey(privateKeyName,
      privateKeyPassword.toCharArray());

  System.out.println("Signing message:\r\n\t" + message);

  byte[] signature = this.getSignature(message.getBytes(), privateKey);

  System.out.println("Verifying signature with the real message.");

  boolean bverify = this.verifySignature(
      message.getBytes(), signature, publicKey);

  if (bverify) {
     System.out.println("SUCCESS: Signature verified.");
  } else {
     System.out.println("ERROR: Signature did not verify.");
  }

  System.out.println("Verifying signature with the fake message:"
      + "\r\n\t" + fakemessage);
```

```
    bverify = this.verifySignature(
        fakemessage.getBytes(), signature, publicKey);

    if (bverify) {
      System.out.println(
        "ERROR: Signature verified with the fake message.");
    } else {
      System.out.println(
        "SUCCESS: Signature did not verify with the fake message.");
    }

    } catch (Exception e) {
      System.out.println("*** Error: " + e);
      e.printStackTrace();
      System.exit(0);
    }
}

public byte[] getSignature(byte[] message, PrivateKey privateKey) {

    try {
      Signature sign = Signature.getInstance(signatureAlgorithm);
      // Initialize the signature object with the private key for
      // signing.

      sign.initSign(privateKey);
      sign.update(message); // feed in the message
      return sign.sign(); // generate the signature
    } catch (Exception e) {
      System.out.println("*** Error: " + e);
      System.exit(0);
    }

    return null;
}

public boolean verifySignature(byte[] message, byte[] signature,
    PublicKey publicKey) {
    try {
      Signature sign = Signature.getInstance(signatureAlgorithm);
      // Initialize the signature object with the public key for
      // verifying.
```

```
        sign.initVerify(publicKey);
        sign.update(message); // test with the signature
        return sign.verify(signature);
    } catch (Exception e) {
        System.out.println("*** Error: " + e);
        System.exit(0);
    }

    return false;
    }
}
```

SignAndVerify Output

```
C:\>java ibm.book.SignAndVerify
Loading the keystore and retrieving keys.
Signing message:
        Lee and McClellan are at Antietam.
Verifying signature with the real message.
SUCCESS:  Signature verified.
Verifying signature with the fake message:
        Lee is at Richmond and McClellan is at Washington.
SUCCESS:  Signature did not verify with the fake message.
```

Conclusion

To make e-business successful, businesses and developers must be able to sign objects to unequivocally state that these objects originated from them. In turn, consumers and users must be able to verify that objects they receive came from their professed owners and arrived without modification. By following the role of public and private keys and specified algorithms, we have demystified the signing and verification process.

When cryptographic messages go bad

When milk goes bad, it's generally easy to tell, as the evidence assaults more than one of our senses. The same holds true for other foods, although cottage cheese may be the rare exception. However, it's not as easy to detect when a cryptographic message has gone sour. These messages are the lifeblood of e-business transactions. Cryptographic messages provide essential guarantees ranging from who sent the message to allowing only the receiver to view the message. So, knowing whether a message is valid or not is of primary importance.

This article sheds light on many of the popular ways in which you or your application can detect whether or not a cryptographic message has indeed gone bad.

Certificates

In previous articles, we discussed the different building blocks of cryptographic messages. An essential part to building a verifiable and secure transaction is the creation of a public and private key for each user. Using a popular key-pair algorithm, such as RSA, users can generate a public and private key pair. Users would squirrel their private key away and ask a Certificate Authority (CA) to bundle their public key along with other identifying attributes into a personal certificate. Next, users would publicize their certificates in a public directory, such as Lightweight Directory Access Protocol (LDAP), thus making the certificate information available to other users who want to verify the authenticity of a message sent by the certificate owner or send the owner secret mail.

A user's public key, packaged in a certificate, and its associated private key are the foundation of today's Public Key Infrastructure (PKI) and popular forms of cryptographic messages. Thus, knowing if a certificate and its associated keys are valid forms the basis of our process to check whether a message remains on the *good* side.

To engage in any form of certificate validity checking, the user or application must have access to a certificate database. This database, for example, can reside on the user's workstation or a network workstation and contain a number of trusted root CA certificates. If they are in the database, the application, user or administrator knows or has previously indicated that any certificate issued by the root CA can be trusted. You can deduce the *certificate chain* of a certificate by following the value of the issuer-distinguished name for a certificate to a matching subject-distinguished name for another certificate, and so forth until you reach a trusted certificate or CA in the certificate database. If you cannot form a chain between the certificate that you are examining to a trusted certificate, either the user or the application must determine whether to add the certificate to the trusted set of certificates. This determination takes place near the end of the certificate check, because a certificate that leads up to a trusted certificate does not automatically mean that the certificate is valid.

Certificate signatures

One of the first things the application should check for is whether or not the signature of the certificate is valid. A signature is a digital fingerprint of data and is unique between different signers of the data. When a CA issues a certificate, the CA takes all the attributes of a certificate and runs the data along with the CA's private key through a signature algorithm, such as MD5withRSA. (The signature algorithm consists of a hash and encryption of the hash.) The result of the operation is a signature value, usually a handful of bytes in comparison to the original size of the data. You can detect whether or not a certificate's signature is valid by taking the signature bytes and the issuer certificate's public key and channeling it through the verification part of the same signature algorithm. If the verification operation returns true, you can be assured that the issuer of the certificate actually created the certificate with all the attributes contained by the certificate.

What happens if verification of a certificate's signature returns false? This could stem from a benign error, such as accidental corruption of the certificate's data in transit, to a more malicious intent, such as someone altering the data of the certificate after it was issued. Whatever the reason, the certificate is bad and should not be trusted.

Certificate Revocation Lists

If the certificate passes the signature verification step, check to see if the certificate is listed on a Certificate Revocation List (CRL). CAs issue CRLs to indicate which of their certificates have been revoked. CRLs include identifying information about the CA and a list of the serial numbers of the revoked certificates. If the certificate is on a CRL, the certificate has been invalidated and should not be trusted. For example, users could have asked their CA to revoke their certificate because they lost their private key or it was compromised.

In current practice, CRLs are not widely used. No popular standard for obtaining CRLs from a CA exists. Users and applications can download CRLs from a CA at periodic intervals, or the CA (such as one on an intranet) can publish its CRLs in a publicly accessible directory. Generally, users are not aware of the CRLs existence and do not have ready access to them, usually because they do not want to take the time and resources to acquire or query information from a set of CAs. So, if CRLs typically are not used for revoking a certificate, what revocation mechanism is used?

Certificate validity period

Users and CAs utilize a certificate's validity period to indicate a bounded time in which the certificate can be used. Start and end dates define the length of a validity period. If the current date falls outside of the validity period, the certificate should be considered invalid or not yet valid. Although many applications provide the customized ability to accept expired certificates, the validity period should not be ignored. A certificate's validity period has become the default way in which certificates get revoked, since CRLs are not widely used. Short validity periods are a way for the CA to force the user to ask for a new certificate. The new certificate could contain the same public key as before. Having a certificate expire after a short to medium interval, such as six months, also allows the user to consider whether or not the next certificate should contain a higher-grade encryption key. A higher-grade key is more impervious to attack.

Certificate checking process

In summary, the following algorithm illustrates a popular way in which you can determine whether or not a certificate is still valid:

1.   Verify the certificate signature.

2.   Check whether the certificate is listed on a CRL.

3.   Ensure the current date falls within the validity period of the certificate.

4.   Trace the certificate to a trusted CA.

This process also is illustrated in **Figure 7.** If these steps are successful, you can relax knowing that you have a valid certificate. This provides sufficient grounds to inspect the rest of the cryptographic message.

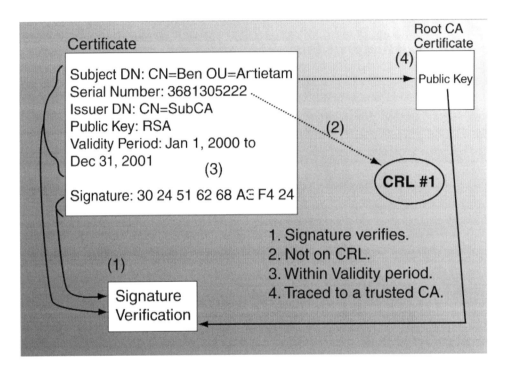

Figure 7: Certificate checking process

Signed messages

In a previous article we also introduced the Public Key Cryptography Standards (PKCS), which defined how cryptographic objects and messages should be packaged. The SignedData object is one of the stars of the PKCS #7 standard. The SignedData object can include the message contents, the certificate of who signed the message, and information about the signer of the message (including the message signature). The SignedData object also was designed so that more than one entity could sign the contents that it contained. When you receive a SignedData message, how can you tell if the message is valid or has gone rancid somewhere in the process?

First, decode the SignedData object and extract its contained objects. Check the set of certificates that it contains using the process discussed earlier. Assuming the certificates are valid, turn to the signature bytes for each signer, since the SignedData object allows more than one entity to sign the contents. Just as you checked with the certificate's signature, use the same algorithm to validate the message signature, feeding the message contents or set of signed attributes, signer's public key (obtained from the signer's certificate), and the signature through the specified signature algorithm. If the signature validation check fails, you have the usual suspects: a garbled message or a nefarious modification. As with an invalid certificate signature, you should not trust this message.

If the message signature validation succeeds, you can take another step to verify the message. Each signer's information contains a signed attribute that indicates when the signature was generated. If the signing time, when the sender signed the message, lies outside of a time period that you define, you can reject the message since the clock skew between the signing time and the current time is too great. Checking the SigningTime attribute is not common but is used for time sensitive applications.

In summary, the following algorithm illustrates a popular way in which you can determine whether or not a signed message is valid:

1.   Validate the certificates.

2.   Verify the signature for each signer.

3.   Optionally check the SigningTime attribute for each signer

Assuming the message passed these steps, you, as the recipient, have assurance that the message originated from the sender and that the message was not altered during transit.

Encrypted messages

When a sender wants to send a secret, encrypted message to a recipient as part of a secure transaction, the sender runs the plain text of the message through a cipher, such as the TripleDES secret key algorithm. However, it would be foolhardy to send the encrypted message and secret key directly to the recipient. The EnvelopedData object, defined in PKCS #7, defines how the secret key should be encrypted with the public key of each recipient. Applications that create an EnvelopedData object, typically generate the secret key on the fly. The EnvelopedData object packages the encrypted contents along with recipient information that includes the encrypted secret key and allows the sender to deliver it to one or more recipients using a standard definition. When you, as the recipient, retrieve the

EnvelopedData message, use your private key to decrypt the secret key and use the secret key to decrypt the content—the end goal.

By themselves, EnvelopedData messages are easy to verify. If recipients can decrypt the message, the recipients know that the message was intended for them. However, this doesn't give the recipient any warm feeling about who sent the message. That is why EnvelopedData objects are usually wrapped around SignedData objects, giving the recipient confidentiality and assurance.

In summary, the following algorithm illustrates a popular way in which you can decrypt and verify a SignedData wrapped EnvelopedData object:

1.   Decrypt the encrypted secret key from the EnvelopedData object using your private key.

2.   Decrypt the encrypted SignedData contents using the secret key.

3.   Verify the SignedData object as before

Note that if the sender and receiver hold the same secret key, the encrypted message could consist of just the encrypted contents. Although it would seem easier to just send encrypted messages without the other attribute baggage, the secret key could be easily compromised since it is held by more than one person and there is no way to verify who sent the message for the same reason. Therein lies the beauty of the SignedData and EnvelopedData objects, which exploit the public and private key technologies.

Conclusion

Certificates and cryptographic messages are fundamental to successful and secure e-business transactions. We've introduced you to various popular ways in which you and your application can ensure the certificates and cryptographic objects can be trusted and haven't gone bad.

Certification paths—Weaving a web of trust

Signed messages play a key role in the security of e-business since they aid in authenticating the sender and ensuring the integrity of messages. However, before one can trust a signed message, the recipient must trust the certificate of the signer. In previous articles, we discussed the importance of the public and private key pair and how they allow signed and encrypted transactions in a scaleable and manageable architecture. This article explorers how the receiver of a signed message can not only ensure that a certificate is valid, but also build a web of trust between certificates to give recipients confidence in the untrustworthy world of the Internet.

Creating Certificates

Each certificate is the public persona of an entity, such as an international corporation or an individual user. A certificate stems from the public debut of an entity's public key generated from a public and private key pair algorithm. In the heart of each certificate rests the entity's public key, publicized for all to see. The private key is kept hidden by the entity to whom the certificate belongs, but by the nature of the public and private key algorithms, the private key is inexorably linked to the public key. The corresponding other key can only decrypt data encrypted by one key.

The other attributes and extensions on the certificate serve to identify the owner of the public key, aid in helping the receiver trace the certificate to its issuer, and determine the role of the certificate. For example, an entity may possess two certificates. The first may be used solely for deciphering encrypted transactions sent to the entity, and the second may be used by the entity to sign transactions. One certificate could have fulfilled both roles, but the certificate architecture is flexible enough to allow a division of roles to conform to the principal of least privileged, for convenience, or for performance purposes.

Knowing the issuer of a certificate plays an important role in building the web of trust. Certificate Authorities (CAs) typically issue certificates in response to an entity's request. A CA may require the approval of a Registration Authority (RA), which authorizes the request. An entity, such as a developer, initiates the request by first generating a public and private key pair. As part of the generation process, the developer specifies the key type and size, such as RSA and 1024. The developer bundles the public key along with identifying information and sends the certification request to either a RA or directly to the CA, bypassing the RA.

Upon receipt of the request and the possible nod of the RA, the CA generates the certificate using attributes the developer sent along with possible additional attributes and extensions that further personify the certificate. The CA generates and sends the certificate back to the developer, who takes the certificate and the associated private key and stores the pair in a protected certificate database, such as the default Java KeyStore implementation or a PKCS #12 file. The CA could also publicize the certificate in a user registry, such as a LDAP database that is available to the entire organization.

Although developers certainly could generate keys and package them, they are more likely to use an application that automatically performs this process for them. Web browsers provide a user-friendly means through which users can generate key pairs and obtain a certificate from a CA. For example, if Benjamin, a developer with Antietam Software, connects to the URL of a CA, completes information on a form, and presses the request certificate button, the browser will create a public and private key pair for Ben and send the public key as part of a PKCS #10 certification request to the CA. If authorization is required, the RA will approve or deny the request. The CA may request the user visit a separate, unique URL after a short period of time to give the RA time to rule on the request.

Assuming that the certificate request was approved, the CA will create the certificate and send it back to the browser in PKCS #7 signed data format, for example. The browser takes the certificate from the PKCS #7 structure and the previously created private key and stores both in a linked relationship in the browser's certificate database. Note that the private key never left the user's workstation, and this safeguard is important to protect the privacy of the private key and the safety of the key owner.

To ensure that the certificate content does not change after the CA issues the certificate, the CA will sign the entire contents of the certificate with a private key of the CA as the final step in the process of creating a certificate. Note that a CA may have more than one public and private key pair at its disposal, depending on whether or not the CA administrator wants to maintain keys at different strengths or wants keys to be used for different geographies. In such cases, a CA would have more than one root certificate. Each root certificate would have the same issuer name, but each would have different public keys.

To sign the certificate, the CA takes an encoding of the contents and the CA's private key and runs both objects through a signature algorithm, such as MD5withRSA. MD5 represents the hash algorithm used to whittle the contents down to a small set of unique bytes. RSA represents the encryption algorithm used to encipher the hash. Verifying the integrity of the certificate requires knowledge of the issuer's public key, which foreshadows the following section of how users trust or obtain pre-trusted certificates, especially those of popular CAs.

There are cases where a certificate may be self-signed. Receivers can recognized self-signed certificates since the subject name and issuer name of the certificate are the same. In practice, self-signed certificates are confined to the realm of testing, since they do not impart trust to the recipient. Anyone can create a self-signed certificate, but only a trusted CA can issue a trusted certificate. Alternatively, users may manually trust certificates, including self-signed certificates that were not issued from a trusted CA.

Trusting Certificates

On the road to building a web of trust, the user (or the user's application) must visit at least four way stations, each with its own ceremony as illustrated in **Figure 8**. The *first way station* is self-contained, but the others require interaction with other objects. When a user receives a signed message along with the certificate of the signer, the user can only perform one type of validation on the certificate without the aid of a certificate database or registry. As part of the certificate attributes, the recipient user can validate the not before and not after dates by checking them against the current date. If the current date falls outside of the validity range, the certificate has expired or is not yet to be trusted. In either case, the certificate is invalid and should not be trusted. If the current date falls with the validity range, the user can continue down the road of weaving a web of trust, but in doing so, needs access to the spool that a certificate database provides.

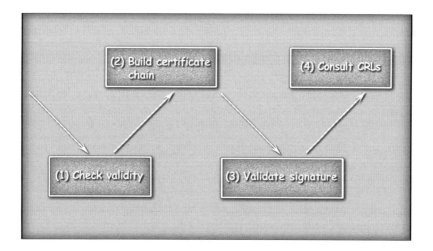

Figure 8: Way stations to weaving a web of trust

Oddly enough, certificate databases do magically appear with most applications and operating systems. These databases are already primed with an initial set of trusted certificates. Before a company releases an application utilizing a public key infrastructure, the application provider typically harvests the public certificates from many of the popular and established CAs. These certificates are known as root certificates, and this sheaf of trusted CA certificates forms the basis of the application's – and hence the user's – trusted certificate database.

With a populated certificate database, the user can travel to the *second way station*, where the user traces the signing certificate to a trusted certificate. The user does this by comparing the issuer name of the signing certificate to the subject name of another certificate in the certificate database. If the two names match, the certificate with the matching subject name is the one who issued the signing certificate. The signing certificate may have come from a trusted root CA certificate or it may have been issued from an intermediary CA whose certificate was issued by a trusted CA certificate. Thus, a certificate chain or path could be short, just two certificates, or long with many certificates, but either case the certificate chain must end with a trusted certificate.

An earlier section discussed how a CA might have more than one root certificate, depending on how the CA administrator wants to manage domains or key sizes. In such cases, the user must compare not only the issuer name of the signing certificate against the subject name of the root CA certificate, but the user must also consult the SubjectKeyIdentifier extension on the signing certificate. The SubjectKeyIdentifier extension contains a hash of the issuer certificate's public key. The user can compute the hash on the public key of each root CA certificate. Once a computed hash matches the value of the SubjectKeyIdentifier extension, the user knows that the right root CA certificate was located.

If the user cannot establish a certificate chain to a trusted certificate, all is not lost. The user's application may ask the user if the certificate should be trusted. If so, the application adds the certificate to the trusted database and continues weaving the web of trust. If not, the certificate and the signed message are branded as untrustworthy. A danger lies in the click syndrome wherein many users tend to press okay when the application presents a dialog box to them without the users fully understanding what the text of the dialog box is saying. This reflexive process could lead to danger if the user accepts a certificate from an untrustworthy source.

The *third way station* brings the signing and issuing certificate into a delicate verification dance. The issuing certificate leads by providing its public key. The signing certificate follows with its encoded contents, signature algorithm, and signature bytes. All this information feeds into the verification process. The verification process, identified by the signature algorithm, first decrypts the signature bytes with the issuer's public key to obtain the decrypted hash. Next, the process generates a hash from the encoded contents. If the generated hash matches the decrypted hash, the user knows that the issuer created the certificate and that no one has tampered with the contents of the certificate since its inception. If the certificate chain consisted of more than one certificate, the user would verify the signature of each certificate in the chain all the way up to the root certificate.

Revoking Certificates

Many times, the journey to building the web of trust ends at the third way station. For completeness, the user's application should escort the certificate to a *fourth way station* where Certificate Revocation Lists (CRLs) come into play. A CA may wish to revoke a certificate for a number of reasons. For example, an employee may separate from a company, so the administrator would need to revoke the certificate issued to the employee by the company's CA. Users may have lost their private key or the private key could have been compromised, and either of these scenarios would mandate that the CA revoke the certificate. Whatever the reason, CAs issue CRLs to indicate that a certificate should not be trusted even though the certificate may still fall within the validity range, be traced to a trusted certificate, and have its original contents intact.

CRLs are not widely used because it is difficult for users to access a current set of CRLs. In the enterprise environment, an administrator may configure a process to automatically poll a set of CAs for their CRLs and populate a public registry with the returned set of CRLs. The user's application could consult this registry or the CRL distribution point extension that may be part of the certificate contents to investigate whether or not the certificate has been revoked. The user checks the serial number of the certificate in question against the set of serial numbers on the CRL matching the issuer of the certificate. If a matching serial number is found, the user knows the certificate has been revoked.

In practice, end users do not widely use CRLs since they may not have access to a CRL repository or do not want to take the time to query CRLs from a CA. Because of this the previous way stations take on added importance in the course of building the web of trust.

Conclusion

Signed messages are an important part of security in the e-business world. (Encrypted messages are important as well, but they alone do not require the establishment of trusted certificate chain.) If recipients or their applications visit all the way stations with the signing certificate in question on the road to building a web of trust, they can have confidence that the signing certificate can be trusted. In doing so, they can use the trusted certificate to complete their goal of verifying their signed message.

Unshackling key management in Java security

As part of building a web of trust in the unsecured world of the Internet, users and developers need to utilize public and private key pairs. These unique key pair combinations give users the ability to sign and encrypt data in an authenticated, verifiable, and secure fashion. Public keys are typically stored in certificate objects, rather than alone. Users and developers may deal with many certificates and may have more than one private key that they use to sign and encrypt or decrypt data. This article reveals an important vault of information in Java security, the KeyStore, which allows users and developers to consolidate and manage their various certificates and keys.

KeyStore Providers

A keystore is a database of private keys and their associated certificates or certificate chains. The certificate chains aid in authenticating end entity certificates. Typically, you have two separate and distinct uses for authentication:

- A need to prove to others who you are.

- A need to make sure others are who they say they are.

The Java Cryptography Architecture (JCA) provides extensible architecture to manage keys. This architecture is embodied in java.security as a KeyStore.

The Java KeyStore follows the existing JCA architecture, which provides a framework and implementations for a KeyStore. The provider architecture of the JCA aims to allow algorithm independence, permitting one vendor to implement a KeyStore in a different fashion than that provided by another vendor. Note that the Java Cryptography Extension (JCE) utilizes the JCA and shares the same philosophy of implementation and algorithm independence by supplying of the provider architecture.

The provider architecture allows different KeyStore implementations. Some of the common implementations that are found today include:

- Flat files,

- PKCS #12 files, and

- Hardware token support.

The default keystore implementation, provided in the reference implementation of Java 2 SDK from Sun, is a flat file and uses a proprietary keystore format. This default implementation is called the Java KeyStore (JKS). The JKS protects the integrity of the entire keystore with a keystore password. A hash value of the entire keystore helps alert the owner if the keystore was altered. Each private key in the keystore is also protected with its own password (though this password may be identical to the keystore password). In different keystore implementations that can make use of encryption, such as the keystore implementation that comes with JCE 1.2.1 from Sun, users have a choice of the encryption algorithm with which they want to store their private keys. The separation of the KeyStore password from the private key password allows more than one user to access the keystore with a shared password, but protects the use of the private key with a password unique to the owner of the private key.

The KeyStore class is provided in the package java.security. It supplies methods to load, modify and save the information in the keystores. The Java 2 SDK provides the *keytool* command to create and manipulate a keystore via the KeyStore APIs. It is possible to change both the implementation and the location of the keystore that comes by default with the Java 2 SDK installation, but users must modify security properties to make the Java system aware of what keystore implementation and location have been selected:

- The implementation of the keystore is specified in the security properties file, defined by the value of the property named keystore.type.

- The location of the keystore is specified in the policy file, defined by the keystore URL entry.

Users and developers can create a new keystore implementation to store keys and certificates in a database, for example. When replacing the default implementation, the new keystore classes must be available and the security properties updated.

In a keystore you can store your own end entity certificates, certificates of Certificate Authorities (CAs), and certificates of other trusted entities. As mentioned earlier, the Java 2 platform provides the *keytool* command line utility for storing private keys and viewing or listing public information about a certificate in a JKS keystore. Since a keystore is password protected, users need to enter a password to access the private information stored in the keystore. If a different password enshrouds the private key, users must enter the secondary password as well.

Note that public information, such as to retrieve a list of all certificates in the keystore, can be accessed without the password. However, in this case, as the keytool utility is unable decrypt the hash and verify the integrity of the keystore, the keytool displays a warning message on the screen.

Sample keytool

```
C:\>keytool  -genkey -alias Tony -keyalg RSA -keysize 1024 -dname "CN=Anthony
Nadalin, OU=Java Security, O=Tivoli, c=US" -keypass tivoli -storepass Tivoli
-keystore c:\test
C:\>
C:\>keytool -list -v -keystore test
Enter keystore password:

*****************  WARNING WARNING WARNING  ****************
* The integrity of the information stored in your keystore  *
* has NOT been verified! In order to verify its integrity,  *
* you must provide your keystore password.                  *
*****************  WARNING WARNING WARNING  ****************

Keystore type: jks
Keystore provider: IBM

Your keystore contains 1 entry:

Alias name: tony
Creation date: Wed Jun 14 15:19:27 CDT 2000
Entry type: keyEntry
Certificate chain length: 1
Certificate[1]:
Owner: CN=Anthony Nadalin, OU=Java Security, O=Tivoli, C=US
Issuer: CN=Anthony Nadalin, OU=Java Security, O=Tivoli, C=US
Serial number: 3947e8cd
Valid from: Wed Jun 14 15:19:25 CDT 2000 until: Tue Sep 12 15:19:25 CDT 2000
Certificate fingerprints:
         MD5:   67:57:DF:4E:5B:26:01:66:9F:33:C2:29:E3:5E:F7:8F
         SHA1:  86:5B:95:9E:0F:33:DB:4E:99:BD:7D:1A:2B:DD:0C:82:40:AE:B4:C3

*******************************************
*******************************************
C:\>
```

If users register the public information of a certificate as trusted and then try to run an applet signed by that certificate, the JVM automatically retrieves the public key from the keystore, without requiring intervention by the user and without prompting for the keystore password. The reason for this is that all public information, such as public key and certificate, is stored unencrypted in the keystore, and only the private key is stored password protected. As mentioned earlier, the secondary password protects the private key, which is essential in signing and decrypting documents, from unauthorized users. The primary password is used for an integrity check only to verify that the keystore has not been tampered with.

The KeyStore holds all this information, organized by aliases or friendly names. Keystore entries are loaded, modified and saved by an alias, similar to the way that Hashtable objects (java.util.Hashtable) work. Users can leverage a single keystore or they can utilize as many as they wish. Creating additional keystores allows users to:

1.   Generate and store a public-private key pair for themselves.

2.   Sign code with their private key and export their certificates in a keystore to send to others to allow verification of their signed code.

3.   Import certificates from other entities to verify signatures.

The keytool command line utility facilitates these actions. As before, the different keystores can be protected with different passwords.

The Default Java Keystore File

The cacerts file is a system-wide keystore for storing trusted CA certificates. It is implemented in the default JKS format, is located in the ${java.home}${/}lib${/}security directory, and can be manipulated with the keytool command line utility.

Currently, the Java 2 SDK ships the cacerts with five VeriSign root CA certificates. Use the -list command associated with the keytool utility to view these certificates.

Sample keytool cacerts

```
C:keytool -list -keystore cacerts

*****************  WARNING WARNING WARNING  ****************
* The integrity of the information stored in your keystore  *
* has NOT been verified! In order to verify its integrity, *
* you must provide your keystore password.                  *
*****************  WARNING WARNING WARNING  ****************

Keystore type: jks
Keystore provider: IBM
```

```
Enter keystore password:
Your keystore contains 10 entries:

verisignclass3ca, Mon Jun 29 12:05:51 CDT 1998, trustedCertEntry,
Certificate fingerprint (MD5): 78:2A:02:DF:DB:2E:14:D5:A7:5F:0A:DF:B6:8E:9C:5D
verisignclass1ca, Mon Jun 29 12:06:17 CDT 1998, trustedCertEntry,
Certificate fingerprint (MD5): 51:86:E8:1F:BC:B1:C3:71:B5:18:10:DB:5F:DC:F6:20
...
```

This command will prompt for the keystore password when launched. However, the password is not mandatory to display the contents of a keystore. Without the password, the output shown in the listing above is displayed with the warning message that the integrity of the information stored in the keystore has not been verified.

The keytool requires users to specify the password to update the database, such as to import a new certificate in the keystore file. By default, the initial password is changeit. As the name itself suggests, users should change the default password, since the keystore contains the certificates of the CAs that are considered trusted. A keystore password can be changed using the -storepasswd command associated with the keytool command line utility.

Since CAs are entities that are trusted by users for signing and issuing certificates to other entities, only system administrators should manage the cacerts file. With the keytool utility, it is possible to add new CA certificates or remove old CA certificates from the cacerts file. Utmost care should be taken while importing any certificate into the cacerts keystore, as it should only contain certificates of the CAs that the system administrator trusts.

Developing with the KeyStore class

The KeyStore class is an abstract class, but developers can obtain a concrete subclass using the getInstance() method. The KeyStore getInstance() method uses the keystore.type java.security property entry to decide what subclass of KeyStore to create. There are two methods that support loading and saving KeyStore objects: load() and store().

Sample keystore load and store

```
...
// get an instance of the "JKS" KeyStore provider
KeyStore ks = KeyStore.getInstance("JKS");
```

```
// load the KeyStore
ks.load(new FileInputStream("testkeys"), "passphrase".toCharArray());
...
// save the KeyStore in the file named "testkeys"
// with a password of "passphrase"
ks.store(new FileOutputStream("testkeys"), "passphrase".toCharArray());
...
```

If you have loaded a particular keystore file and want to store a key pair, you would add the private key and the certificate that represents the corresponding public key to the keystore. You could also add the chain of certificates linking the certificate to a trusted CA. This can be accomplished via the setKeyEntry() method.

Sample keystore isKeyEntry…

```
// See if we have a key or a certificate and make the appropriate KeyStore
call
if (ks.isKeyEntry(alias)) {
    newEntry = new KeyEntry(alias, ks.getCertificateChain(alias),
        ks.getKey(alias, passChars) );
} else if (ks.isCertificateEntry(alias)) {
    newEntry = new CertificateEntry(alias, ks.getCertificate(alias));
}
...
```

To retrieve entries from a KeyStore you may use one of several methods: getPrivateKey(), getCertificateChain(), or getCertificate().

Conclusion

This article discussed the architecture and current implementation of key management in Java 2 Standard Edition, Version 1.2, from Sun. Along with the addition of other packages, public key technologies are becoming an essential part of the Java security architecture, and we expect that the pace of integration will continue to accelerate.

Internet Security

In this section, we discuss broader security topics, including how to understand cryptographic messages over the Internet and identifying the essential Java packages to creating robust e-business Web sites. We also dive into the Secure Socket Layer (SSL) and its availability in Java security. SSL and its successor, Transport Layer Security (TLS), are crucial to building a secure e-business Web site in the insecure world of the Internet.

- Understanding cryptographic messages

- Harvesting the essential Java security features

- Exploiting SSL in Java security

- Exploiting SSL in Java security, Part II

Understanding cryptographic messages

This article takes the building blocks of certificates and signatures and demonstrates how they are used in today's e-business transactions. In particular, this article introduces the Public Key Cryptography Standards (PKCS) and the use of the signed data in Secure/Multipurpose Internet Mail Extensions (S/MIME) transactions.

Certificates are a unique and standard way in which users and entities can publicly represent themselves in electronic commerce. When users have certificates, they have placed information about themselves, such as their name and e-mail address, in the public domain with a way for that information to be verified or revoked. A certificate also can contain the user's or entity's public key, and this key plays an integral role in the signature process.

The signature process utilizes the user's public key and associated private key to provide for the verification of data. A key pair algorithm uses a random value or other seed to generate a public and private key pair. A user can sign data, such as a message, by running the data through a signature algorithm that also takes the associated private key. The recipient of the data and signature can verify the signature value by running the signature, data and the user's public key through the verification algorithm, which is the counterpart to the signature algorithm. If the algorithm returns true for verification, the recipient knows that the data originated from the sender and that it was not modified in transit.

Public-Key Cryptography Standards (PKCS)

RSA Security Inc. and a consortium of companies developed the first pieces of PKCS in 1991. The set of PKCS standards has expanded and matured to encompass everything from defining encryption techniques (PKCS #1 and #5) to the use of smartcards and electronic tokens (PKCS #11 and #15). The standards include PKCS #7, which describes how signed and encrypted data should be presented, and PKCS #8, which defines the format for private keys, including encrypted private keys. PKCS #9 defines a set of attributes used by many of the PKCS standards. When users request a certificate from a Certificate authority (CA), they send their public key in a PKCS #10 object to the CA and, once approved, the CA issues a certificate that is wrapped in a PKCS #7 object.

PKCS #12 defines a format for packaging various objects together in a single file. For example, when users export a certificate from a Web browser's certificate database, the Web browser typically creates a password-protected PKCS #12 file containing the exported certificate and accompanying private key. PKCS #12 files are meant to be interchangeable, allowing them to be imported into another Web browser or system certificate database.

Most Internet and intranet transactions are conducted using one or more of the PKCS standards. A good user interface shields users from needing to know that PKCS standards and objects are being used under the covers, but be assured, they play a key roll in ensuring that transactions can be verified and kept secret. In particular, most e-business transactions exploit objects defined by PKCS #7.

PKCS #7: Cryptographic message syntax standard

The PKCS #7 standard includes a host of widely used objects. The most popular objects include EnvelopedData and SignedData. The EnvelopedData object allows senders to encrypt data with a secret key. (Typically, the application that creates the EnvelopedData object automatically creates the secret key so that the caller does not need to generate it.) The secret key also is encrypted for each recipient, using the recipient's public key. Once the EnvelopedData object arrives, each recipient can use the private key to decrypt the secret key, which in turn can be used to decrypt the data. Popular encryption algorithms include RC2, DES and Triple DES.

The SignedData object allows senders to package and sign data and recipients to verify the signed data. This object contains a number of attributes and subobjects. The top layer is composed of the digest algorithm, encapsulated contents, a set of certificates and a set of Certificate Revocation Lists (CRLs). Applications can use CRLs to determine that the certificates are still valid and have not been revoked by the issuing CA. A set of SignerInfo objects forms the second layer. Each SignerInfo object includes the issuer and serial number corresponding to a certificate in the parent SignedData certificate set, the digest and signature algorithms, signed and unsigned attributes, and the signature value itself. Popular digest and signature algorithms include SHA1withDSA and MD5withRSA.

Note that not all fields are required. For example, CRLs are rarely packaged with SignedData objects. Additionally, the SignedData object is structured to allow more than one user or entity to sign the data. A SignerInfo object represents each signer. No matter how many users sign the data, the SignedData object does not replicate the data to be signed. It is enclosed once at the top layer in the encapsulated contents.

Different types of signed data

The fact that not all fields are required means that applications can use the SignedData object in a variety of forms. The first form a SignedData object can take packages the signed contents and at least one signature. When populated with contents and one or more SignerInfo objects, recipients of the SignedData object can verify that the content was signed by the certificate corresponding to the SignerInfo object.

Frequently, senders construct the SignedData object without contents and wind up sending the contents along with the separate SignedData object to recipients. This second form is known as a signature-only SignedData object. The signature-only object contains the signature value and information about the signer to allow recipients to take these values along with the detached message and verify the signature normally. Recipients cannot use the SignedData object itself to verify the signature on each SignerInfo object since the verification algorithm requires the detached contents to be included as part of its parameters.

The third most popular form of the SignedData object is known as certificate-only. Earlier, we discussed how users could send a PKCS #10 message to a CA to request a certificate. In response, the CA can send back a certificate-only SignedData object. This object only contains a certificate; it does not contain any contents or SignerInfo objects, since there were no contents to sign.

The PKCS #7 standard allows objects to be wrapped within other objects. For example, a user can seal a message by first signing the message by creating a SignedData object. Next, the user can encrypt the SignedData object by creating an EnvelopedData object that takes the SignedData object as its contents to encrypt. To unseal, recipients would decrypt the sealed object to gain access to the SignedData and verify the signature for each of the SignerInfo objects contained in the SignedData object before extracting the message enclosed within.

The PKCS #7 standard has continued to evolve. The most recent version of the standard is reflected in RFC 2630. This version upgrades the objects and attributes to support additional functionality.

Sending signed data

Let's say that Ben wants to use his e-mail application to send a signed message to his business colleague, Patrick, who lives near Antietam creek. All Ben needs to do is compose the message and select the signed message checkbox before pressing the send button. When Patrick receives the message, his e-mail application displays the message along with an icon indicating that the message was signed and verified. Patrick can rest assured that Ben sent the message and that the contents were not tampered with in transit.

Sending signed data is a simple process for the user, but this process is more complicated under the graphical interface. Developers of e-mail programs and any application that sends and receives signed data need to be involved in the intricacies of the signing and verification process.

Before delving into the details of the transaction, let's first examine the use of S/MIME. To send secure messages between parties, developers have created the S/MIME standard, which extends the MIME standard. The S/MIME standard builds upon the PKCS standards to allow applications to send secure data through such public mail protocols as the Simple Mail Transfer Protocol (SMTP). Today's applications implement version 2 of the S/MIME specifications. Work on the version 3 specifications currently is underway.

S/MIME Version 2 builds upon the PKCS #7 and #10 objects. The MIME file extensions convey the types of supported objects:

- p7m – EnvelopedData or SignedData with contents

- p7s – SignedData with signature(s) only

- p7c – SignedData with certificate(s) only

- p10 – CertificationRequest object

S/MIME further wraps the SignedData and EnvelopedData objects in a PKCS #7 ContentInfo object that consists of the content type and content fields. The ContentInfo object helps senders package the different PKCS #7 objects in a common object. The content type field helps recipients to identify the transmitted object and use the content field to decode it.

Figure 9 shows how an application, such as an e-mail program, signs and sends Ben's message to Patrick. Once Ben composes his message and presses the send button, the application extracts Ben's private key from the application's keystore or certificate database. The application feeds the private key and message into the signing algorithm, such as MD5withRSA, and generates a signature. This signature, along with other information, is bundled into a signature-only SignedData object. Before sending the message, the application constructs a p7s S/MIME message with MIME header information, original message and SignedData object.

MIME header information includes such information as the content transfer encoding, which is BASE64 for PKCS objects. Finally, the application sends the S/MIME message to Patrick via SMTP.

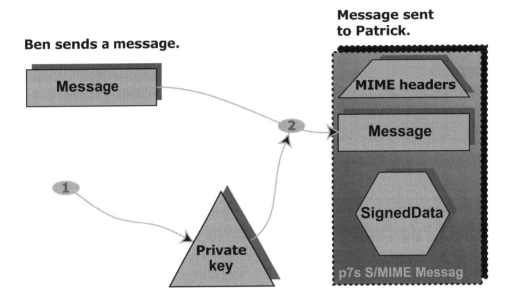

1. **Application extracts Ben's private key from the certificate or keystore database.**
2. **Application signs the message with Ben's private key, creates a p7s multipart S/MIME message, and sends it to Patrick.**

Figure 9: Sending a signed message

Figure 10 shows how Patrick's application receives and verifies Ben's message. The application first verifies the MIME headers in the S/MIME message. If the headers indicate a pkcs7-signature type, the application extracts the certificate corresponding to each SignerInfo from the SignedData object and verifies it by tracing the certificate chain back to a trusted root CA. If the certificate is verified, the application extracts the public key from the certificate and extracts the signature(s) from the SignerInfo objects in the SignedData object. The application verifies each signature with the message and corresponding public key, returning true or displaying the signed and verified graphic if the verification was successful.

Sending a p7s detached signature message allows recipients who do not have S/MIME enabled e-mail applications to view the contents of the message even though they are not able to verify the integrity and authenticity of the message.

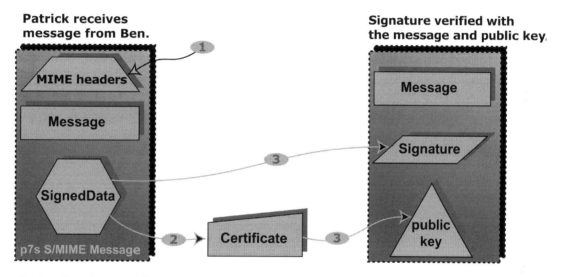

1. Application verifies the MIME headers.
2. Application extracts and verifies the certificate.
3. Application extracts the signature and verifies it with the message and the public key from the certificate.

Figure 10: Receiving and verifying a signed message

Conclusion

This article discussed the popular cryptographic message standards, PKCS and S/MIME, that are in use today. Using PKCS objects to sign data is not limited to e-mail. Applications can sign and encrypt various formats of binary data in all types of e-business transactions, particularly those that travel across public networks. A developer's mastery of these underlying standards helps customers focus on their business objectives without having to know the infrastructure details that keep their transactions safe and secure.

Harvesting the essential Java security features for e-business

The articles in this book have provided a wealth of Java security information. We began with the fundamentals of the security model in the Java Runtime Environment (JRE), such as protection domains, and worked towards an understanding of the Java Cryptography Architecture (JCA) and its features, such as representing certificate objects and signing data. Articles on the Java Cryptography Extension (JCE) built upon our prior knowledge and showed encryption in action. We provided an introduction to the Public Key Cryptography Standards (PKCS) and Java Secure Socket Extension (JSSE), which harnessed the vigor of these lower level technologies at a higher, more manageable level.

These popular e-business technologies have been scattered about in different Java packages from various vendors, and developers have sheaved them together to gain the breath of Java security functionality that enterprise applications require. This article describes the general capabilities of the popular Java security packages. **Figure 11** provides a preview of the Java security features showcased in this article.

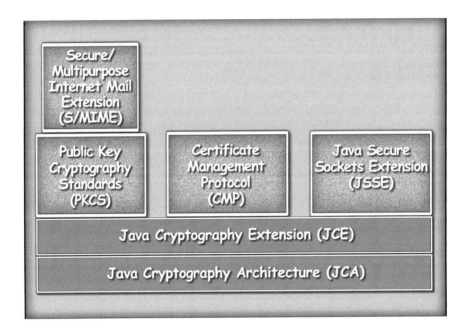

Figure 11: Essential Java security layers

Building a Security Foundation

The foundation of the vast majority of Java security is poured by the Java Cryptography Architecture (JCA) and hardened by the Java Cryptography Extension (JCE). The JCA provides representations of the essential objects for modeling security. They include rendering the public and private key pair objects and certificates. Certificates represent the debut of public keys in a standard format that includes additional attributes, such as the subject name and validity period of the certificate. The JCA provides an implementation for the most popular format – X.509.

A successful e-business solution must address the security requirements for the most popular Internet commerce scenarios:

1.   Sending a message wherein the sender can be authenticated and whose message integrity can be verified.

2. Exchanging confidential information with a recipient through encryption and decryption of the message or transaction.

3. Publicizing information about oneself in a trusted manner.

Public and private key technologies address all these requirements. Public and private keys are unique in that data encrypted with one key can only be decrypted with the other key. The process of signing a message and verifying the signature bytes for a message involves public and private keys. Given their inherent nature, both keys also can play a role in encryption. Lastly, certificates provide entities, such as a person (e.g., Benjamin the software engineer) or corporation (e.g., Antietam Software), a standard method in which public keys for the entities can be represented and stored in a trusted fashion. Certificates allow users to build a web of trust from a signing certificate to a trusted root Certificate Authority (CA), for example.

JCE provides the other half of the security equation – the confidentiality and integrity provided by encryption and hashing. Among other objects, the JCE provides secret keys and their accompanying cipher objects. Secret keys operate differently from public and private keys in that only one key is used to encrypt and decrypt data. Although secret keys fail to provide a solution for key distribution, cipher algorithms that use secret keys can encrypt and decrypt bulk data much faster than public and private keys.

As we will learn, public and private key pairs and secret keys can be used in combination to provide more complex solutions to e-business problems.

Both the JCA and JCE provide a framework in which various service providers can plug-in different implementations of existing algorithms, as well as entirely new algorithms, such as the cipher implementation for the upcoming Advanced Encryption Standard (AES), which will replace the Data Encryption Standard (DES).

The recent release of JCE 1.2.1 allows the framework to be exported outside of the United States. Prior to JCE 1.2.1, the framework did not have a way to distinguish between localities and thus it could not provide its entire suite of cryptographic functionality internationally. With JCE 1.2.1, service providers can go through the process of getting their implementations signed and shipped worldwide – though they are still bound by U.S. export regulations that include prohibitions on exporting to embargoed countries. The jurisdiction policy file governs which cryptographic algorithms and strengths are available to customers in the target territory.

Exploiting Public Key Technologies

The JCA and JCE provide the basis for fundamental security operations: signing, encryption, and publication. These primary objects and functionality are useful in themselves, but they can be aggregated and expanded in a standard fashion to allow more complex solutions. The Public Key Cryptography Standards (PKCS) give developers the formal standards to bring the public key technologies to the next level.

RSA and a consortium of companies crafted PKCS as a handful of standards in the early 1990s. Since then, the standards have grown to cover everything from encryption to object packaging, yet the public key warms at the hearth of this family of standards. Some of the most popular standards include #1, #5, #7, #8, #9, #10, and #12. In the Java world, PKCS implementations are heavy users of the architecture and objects provided by the JCA and JCE.

PKCS #1: RSA Cryptography Standard

There are two popular types of public key algorithms: DSA and RSA. DSA private keys cannot be used to encrypt general data, although they can be used to sign messages and this process involves encrypting the hash of the data. RSA provides a more general-purpose encryption solution, and this standard covers how to use RSA public and private keys for encryption.

PKCS #5: Password-Based Cryptography Standard

PKCS #5 is similar to PKCS #1 in that it provides for encryption, but not with public keys. PKCS #5 uses passwords instead, and although not directly related to public keys, the algorithms introduced in PKCS #5 are used by other PKCS standards that utilize or store private keys, such as encrypting private key objects with a password.

PKCS #7: Cryptographic Message Syntax Standard

A simple security operation, such as signing a message, requires many attributes and objects. To name just a few, the signer and verifier of the message must know the signature algorithm, signer's certificate, original message, and signature bytes. PKCS #7 describes how to package this information together in a standard fashion, allowing senders to encode the objects and receivers to decode the information in a predictable, interoperable way.

This standard covers a variety of compound objects, including SignedData and EnvelopedData, which are used for sending signed or encrypted data to recipients in a trusted manner. These objects can wrap each other, providing even more flexibility and functionality. For example, a message can be sealed, which involves creating a SignedData object with the data that in turn is encrypted within an EnvelopedData object. After decrypting and verifying the message, the recipient of a sealed message gets the security guarantees of both the signing and encryption processes, not just one or the other.

PKCS #8: Private-Key Information Syntax Standard

Public keys are meant to be shared freely. Certificates bear them for the world to view since they are key to the verification process. Private keys, on the other hand, are meant to be hidden. Owners of private keys should not store them unguarded for others to causally view or maliciously use. PKCS #8 provides standard definitions for encoding and decoding private keys either in raw form or, preferably, in an encrypted format.

PKCS #9: Selected Attribute Types

With all the objects that the various PKCS standards introduce, there are many common attributes, such as ContentType and MessageDigest. PKCS #9 defines these attributes and more. For example, default implementations of SignerInfo used the aforementioned attributes and the SigningTime attribute, which indicates when the owner of the signing certificate signed the message contents. Before becoming part of its parent SignedData object, the SignerInfo object signs these attributes with the signer's private key to ensure their authentication and integrity to the eventual recipients of the SignedData object.

PKCS #10: Certification Request Syntax Standard

Public keys form the basis of certificates, and CAs create certificates, but how can a user request a certificate? PKCS #10 provides a popular way to request certificates from a CA. In the beginning, the user, typically through a key generator in an application like a Web browser, creates a public and private key pair. The Web browser squirrels the private key away and bundles the public key and accompanying attributes into a PKCS #10 object, which is then sent to the CA as the formal certification request.

Interestingly, the CA leverages the PKCS #7 standard to send back the generated certificate to the user's Web browser within a SignedData object. The browser takes the certificate and associated private key and stores both into the browser's certificate database.

PKCS #12: Personal Information Exchange Syntax Standard

PKCS #12 provides for the bundling of various object information into one object. Although PKCS #12 objects can be used for a variety of applications, Web browsers use this standard to export a certificate and its associated private key in a confidential fashion. The user can import the created PKCS #12 file import into a different certificate database, such as that belonging to a user directory or another Web browser database. Since the file includes the sensitive private key, users can encrypt and thus protect the PKCS #12 file with a public key, such as those derived from the RSA algorithm, or with a password, leveraging the PKCS #5 standard.

Sending Secure Messages

The Multipurpose Internet Mail Extensions (MIME) provide an extensible standard to send messages and data across the Internet. MIME messages, however, lack security guarantees, which would be essential to flow confidential data across the unsecured pathways of the Internet. The Secure/Multipurpose Internet Mail Extensions (S/MIME) specifications remedy this by building upon the PKCS #7 objects to provide signing and encryption to MIME messages. The specifications also provide support for PKCS #10 Certification Request objects. In the Java world, S/MIME utilizes the Java implementations of PKCS #7 and #10.

Requesting Certificates

The PKCS section describes two standards that users and developers can exploit as part of the certificate generation process. PKCS #10 provides a means to request a certificate from the CA, and the CA uses the PKCS #7 SignedData object to return the created certificate. This coupling of standards works well in a stateless, asynchronous environment, but complex environments that require synchronous and more easily auditable transactions require a more robust mechanism.

The Certificate Management Protocol (CMP) is a cornerstone of the Public Key Infrastructure X.509 (PKIX). The CMP describes a protocol wherein an End Entity (EE), such as a user, can communicate with a CA and vice versa. Oftentimes, the certification request process involves a Registration Authority (RA) to decide whether or not the CA can generate a certificate for the EE. CMP is robust enough for the CA and RA to communicate with each other. The PKCS standards lack this built-in support.

As one can guess, since CMP involves public and private keys and the signing of information as part of creating a certificate, CMP utilizes the JCA within the Java realm.

Ensuring a Secure Transaction

A last essential piece to a vigorous suite of Java security features is the ability to establish a secure connection between two entities. The Java Secure Sockets Extension (JSSE) accomplishes this by implementing the Secure Sockets Layer (SSL) and Transport Layer Security (TLS). Popularized by Netscape, SSL provides a means for two entities, such as user at a client Web browser and a business at a Web server, to communicate with each other in an authenticated and encrypted fashion. In the Java world, JSSE exploits both the JCA and JCE.

The SSL process begins with public keys, but quickly sets them aside in favor of a secret key. The client and server begin with an already established public or private key pair or generate them as necessary. After using the key pairs to authenticate each other, the client and server begin a meticulous dance wherein they agree upon a secret key. As described earlier, secret keys are more efficient at encrypting and decrypting, thus once established, the client and server use the secret key to exchange confidential information between themselves.

Conclusion

This article introduces the popular and essential Java security features. The JCA and JCE provide the foundation for representing the fundamental security objects and actions. Java implementations of PKCS, S/MIME, CMP, and SSL leverage the JCA and JCE to gain more complex capability.

Exploiting SSL in Java security

Introduction

The Secure Sockets Layer (SSL) is the network protocol that provides data privacy for the bulk of the browser-to-Web server e-business applications that exist on the Internet today. This article gives a background on SSL itself, discusses the Java Secure Sockets Extension (JSSE), and exercises one of its higher-level application programming interfaces through an example.

Origins of SSL

SSL was first developed by Netscape to provide secure data transmission to and from Netscape Web browsers and Netscape Web servers over the insecure links that make up the Internet. SSL has been highly successful and widely adopted, either in its original form as documented by Netscape, or in a more standardized form from the Internet Engineering Task Force (IETF), known as Transport Layer Security (TLS). This article focuses on SSL, but much of what is discussed pertains as well to TLS.

SSL has gone through several different versions. As with most engineering efforts, the first version that was widely accepted and used was Version 2. Version 3 added several key features to V2 that made it a highly desirable update, the most notable being support for client certificates and session caching.

Key Features of SSL

There are three features of SSL that deserve attention:

(1) Data privacy

One of the primary features of SSL is that all data transmitted via SSL is encrypted so that casual observers cannot read the information. In addition, SSL can also detect tampering with the data, so users on both sides of the connection will know if anything was changed in transit. This sort of tamper-proof confidentiality is a prerequisite for being able to exchange sensitive data like credit card information on the Internet.

(2) Server authentication

To be able to provide encrypted data transmission, a cryptographic key must be known by both the sending and receiving parties (and hopefully, by no one else!). Distributing this key to everyone who needs it (and no one else) is one of the challenges of practical cryptography. Application architectures would like to use symmetric secret-key cryptography, because of its speed, but key distribution and vulnerability to attack along the path of distribution are two problems that would need to be solved. Asymmetric public key cryptography would permit easier and more secure key distribution, but by its nature, public key cryptography generally makes for slower cryptography.

SSL finesses these issues by using both methods of cryptography: secret key and public key. SSL uses public key technology early in the establishment of a client's session with a server. Near the end of session establishment, the SSL protocol provides for both parties to generate a secret key starting with the same starting values, exchanged over an already-encrypted communication line, and using an agreed-upon secret-key algorithm. Thus SSL gets the benefit of speedy cryptography for the bulk of the data transfer, and avoids the vulnerabilities of secret-key distribution.

SSL still has the problem of providing enough infrastructure to be able to do public-key cryptography on both sides of the connection. Along with the necessary cryptography code, on the client side, the client program will need to know which certificate authorities (CAs) it should trust, and on the server side, the server process will need a certificate that asserts the owning organization's identity, as proved by a digital signature from a particular CA. Thus, SSL usually provides some root certificates for the CAs that it will consider trusted and bundles these certificate into a file that is distributed to both the client and server sides. Additionally, the server must obtain a certificate from a CA from the trusted CA set that will identify the server machine as being part of the corporate entity that purchased the Web server certificate from the CA.

With that background, applications can start an SSL connection. As part of the exchange that goes on when the client attempts to connect to the server, the server's certificate is sent to the client. The client looks to see if it has a certificate in its trusted certificate database that matches the issuer of the server certificate. If not or if the client cannot trace the server certificate through a certificate chain to a trusted certificate, the client ends the SSL connection. If the client doesn't have a server certificate that it can trust, the SSL session cannot be established.

Assuming the client has the issuer certificate in its list of trusted CAs, the client verifies the signature on the server certificate and checks the domain specified in the server certificate against the server's current address. If these values are valid, the client has authenticated the server and can use the server's public key to protect the rest of the session setup.

(3) Client authentication

Although not required by the SSL protocol, the client may have a certificate of its own with which it wishes to identify itself. At this point in the session establishment, the client must present that certificate to the server. Now it's the server's turn to do some soul-searching about whether it can trust the certificate that the client is presenting. If the server cannot accept the client's certificate-based identity, the server will close the SSL session with an error.

If either the server accepted the client's certificate or the client had no certificate to present, the client side and the server side will jointly compute a secret key based on data that the client computed and forwarded to the server after encrypting the data under the server's public key. With the secret key in hand by both parties, SSL has successfully established a connection. Whew! It's important to note that a fair amount of processing went into this session establishment, so it's not a trivial thing to set up and tear down SSL connections. Early users of SSL noted this, so SSL Version 3 protocol provides optional session caching so that a *closed* session might be re-used, still not for free, but with some savings. Version 3 also re-worked the network flows to make them more efficient.

Java Secure Sockets Extension (JSSE)

Although SSL has been very successful as a network protocol, the APIs were never publicly documented for programmer use, which limited its usefulness and acceptance to the browser-to-Web-server world from which it originated. JSSE takes the usefulness of SSL and adds it to the extensive collection of tools in the Java programmer's toolbox.

The Java platform and the Internet and SSL all grew up in the same neighborhood, so they go back a long ways together. Early on, the Java Server Toolkit (JST) made an implementation of SSL available in the javax.net.ssl package. More recently, Sun published JSSE as a standard extension to the Java 2 Standard Edition (J2SE). This extension is completely written in the Java language and exploits the J2SE security model.

Https Handler

The easiest way to start making use of JSSE is to use the https protocol handler that JSSE supplies. For those who are trying to place this particular acronym, https is simply the Hypertext Transfer Protocol (http, the lingua franca of the Web) over an SSL socket. The Java platform provides a number of interesting services that allow easy interaction with Web servers, and the https handler is an extension that allows programs to do this over SSL.

UseHttps.java

```java
package ibm.book;

import java.io.BufferedReader;
import java.io.InputStreamReader;
import java.io.IOException;
import java.net.*;
import java.security.Security;
import java.util.Properties;

public class UseHttps {

    public static void main(String argv[]) {

        Class factoryClass = null;
        URLStreamHandlerFactory factory = null;
        String socksServer = "";
        String socksPort = "";
        String usage = "Usage: java UseHttps URL-to-be-read"
            + " socksServerName(optional) socksPortNumber(optional)";

        if ((argv == null) || (argv.length == 0)) {
            System.out.println(usage);
            return;
        }

        String prefix = "https://";
        // Build the complete URL, including the protocol
        String fullURL = prefix.concat(argv[0]);

        if (argv.length > 3) {
            System.out.println(usage);
            return;
        }

        if (argv.length >= 2) {
            socksServer = argv[1];
            if (argv.length == 3) {
                socksPort = argv[2];
            }
        }
```

```
        System.out.println("Computed URL is " + fullURL);

// Now either we can rely on the user to have added us to
// the security.provider list in java.security, or we can
// dynamically add ourselves here. We'll set it up here.

Security.addProvider(new com.sun.net.ssl.internal.ssl.Provider());

Properties properties = System.getProperties();

String handlers = System.getProperty("java.protocol.handler.pkgs");
if (handlers == null) {
   // nothing specified yet (expected case)
   properties.put("java.protocol.handler.pkgs",
      "com.sun.net.ssl.internal.www.protocol");
} else {
   // something already there, put ourselves out front
   properties.put("java.protocol.handler.pkgs",
      "com.sun.net.ssl.internal.www.protocol|".concat(handlers));
}

if (!socksServer.equals("")) {
   // Must do the setup to get to the socks host
   // Could check first to see if the user already specified it
   // on the invocation line
   if (System.getProperty("socksProxyHost") == null) {
      properties.put("socksProxyHost", socksServer);
   }
   if (!socksPort.equals("")) {
      if (System.getProperty("socksProxyPort") == null) {
         properties.put("socksProxyPort", socksPort);
      }
   }
}

// put the updated properties back in System
System.setProperties(properties);
try {
   // Process the URL far enough to find the right handler
   URL page = new URL(fullURL);
   URLConnection urlc = page.openConnection();
   urlc.setUseCaches(false); // Don't look at possibly cached data
```

```
        // See what's here
        System.out.println("Content-type = " + urlc.getContentType());
        // See how much of it there is
        System.out.println("Content-length = " + urlc.getContentLength());
        // Read it all and print it out
        BufferedReader br = new BufferedReader(
            new InputStreamReader(urlc.getInputStream()));
        String buffer = "\n";
        while (buffer != null) {
            try {
                System.out.println(buffer);
                buffer = br.readLine();
            }
            catch (IOException ioe) {
                ioe.printStackTrace();
                break;
            }
        }
    }
    catch (MalformedURLException mue) {
        System.out.println(fullURL + " is not a URL that can be resolved");
    }
    catch (IOException ie) {
        ie.printStackTrace();
    }
  }
}
```

Once the handler is in place, applications can make use of HttpURLConnection or URLConnection methods and services, and all this will flow over an SSL socket. To illustrate, the sample program, UseHttps.java, if launched as follows:

```
java  ibm.book.UseHttps  bigcitybank.com
```

will read the contents of an SSL-protected page at the Big City Bank. Of course, there are some setup details that the program has to tend to first. For one, J2SE has to be able to find the JSSE jars (jsse.jar, jnet.jar, and jcert.jar), so they need to be added to the CLASSPATH. The bulk of JSSE functionality is in jsse.jar, but the factory classes in jnet.jar and the certificate support in jcert.jar make them required pieces as well.

You will notice that the program accepts two additional parameters, socksProxyHost and socksProxyPort. Users could specify these parameters to run this application behind a socks-enabled firewall. For example, to run this application inside a company's firewall, specify:

```
java  UseHttps bigcitybank.com  socks.company.com
```

and take the default socksProxyPort setting of port 1080. If the reader chooses to run the application at home, using a normal Internet Service Provider (ISP), these parameters will not be necessary.

The next thing to notice is the dynamic adding of another cryptographic provider. JSSE comes with its own cryptographic provider, but the cryptography framework must be told to use it. Users or administrators could edit the java.security file to add this additional provider, but this sample program hardcodes the provider name instead.

The next thing to notice is the setting up of the https protocol handler. A *protocol* is the first part of the URL, the part to the left of the colon, so in " https://bigcitybank.com", it's the "https" part. Sun documents how to add protocol handlers to the URL support that J2SE already provides (http, ftp, mailto, jar, etc), but this information is somewhat hidden in the documentation for a particular constructor in the java.net.URL class. The documentation specifies that J2SE will parse the system property java.protocol.handler.pkgs for package names, to which J2SE will append ".Handler" and J2SE will try to load a class by that name. If the class is found and is a subclass of URLStreamHandler, then it will be used to handle streams of that type. What this sample program is doing is simply not relying on the user to have specified:

```
java -Djava.protocol.handler.pkgs=com.sun.net.ssl.internal.www.protocol
     bigcitybank.com
```

which seems more than a bit ungainly. Since this sample program already had the potential to change the system properties to reflect the socks information, this seemed like a helpful addition to make.

And that's about it for the example. The rest is just the mechanics of downloading the page and printing it to the screen. If this application were part of a scripting of pages from the Big City Bank, it would be easy to fish relevant information out of this page and drive subsequent flows programmatically rather than through a browser.

Of course, there are many more APIs available in JSSE, but a full discussion of all of them is beyond the scope of this article. The https handler is a relatively high-level API that provides a lot of function with very little effort and illustrates well the leverage that Java security gives users in secure distributed computing.

Note that there is an area that neither SSL nor JSSE 1.0 address very well. The mechanisms by which one might manage the certificates necessary to begin an SSL session are largely unspecified, and because they are unspecified, implementations will need to provide their own, possibly proprietary, possibly platform-specific, likely non-interoperable mechanisms to have complete, viable products. For example, different SSL implementations may use different key ring formats to store their certificates. When this shortcoming is addressed, perhaps in a future versions of JSSE, the impact and longevity of JSSE will be assured.

Summary

SSL has been highly successful in secure transmission of sensitive data. It makes wise use of both secret and public key encryption technologies, and is likely to continue to see wide usage on the Web. JSSE takes SSL a step further and makes the standard Java APIs available to Java programmers to create a powerful combination indeed.

Exploiting SSL in Java security, Part II

Introduction

In our previous article on the Secure Sockets Layer (SSL) in Java security, we covered the fundamentals of SSL and how developers can utilize the common features of SSL through the Java Secure Sockets Extension (JSSE) and its support for the Secure Hypertext Transport Protocol (HTTPS). This article probes more deeply into the JSSE package itself and illustrates how developers can avail themselves of the socket-level programming that JSSE also offers. As before, this article focuses on the level of JSSE that is currently available, JSSE 1.0.

Structure

JSSE is structured as a combination of a set of framework classes, and then a set of implementation classes that slides in under the framework to make the package come alive. The framework classes form the public API to which developers are supposed to write their applications, and if the extension has been well architected, developers will never have to pay any attention to the implementation classes themselves. From a developer's point of view, this modularity allows a user or administrator to substitute at run-time a JSSE implementation from another vendor (better performance, stronger cryptography, etc.) without having to make any changes to applications that make use of these services.

Framework classes

The framework classes are located in packages that start with javax. The packages include javax.net, javax.net.ssl, and javax.security.cert.

The classes in javax.security.cert are not central to the job at hand, but they contain an X.509 certificate implementation that is more suitable to JSSE than that offered by the java.security.cert package in the Java 2 Standard Edition (J2SE), so this package does not need any further elaboration.

The javax.net package contains just two abstract classes: SocketFactory and ServerSocketFactory. The difference between a Socket and a ServerSocket is that a ServerSocket expects to start communications by receiving packets, whereas a Socket expects to transmit first. The Factory is a class that expects to produce items of a particular type. Furthermore, the Factory exists to encapsulate details of production of items of this type. To illustrate, a particular implementation of a SocketFactory may produce sockets that know how to traverse a particular firewall, or that may have certain cryptographic characteristics.

Both SocketFactory and ServerSocketFactory contain default implementations that construct normal, non-SSL sockets, so although these classes are abstract, the getDefault() static method will return a reference to an inner class that is an implementation that users can use for normal sockets. The intent here is to allow an application to utilize different types of sockets without knowing much about how the magic happens. Being able to use different types of sockets may not seem terribly novel, but previous incarnations of SSL for Java security would not permit multiple types of sockets to be used in an application, so this is actually a big improvement. Our sample program below will make use of this capability. With the preliminaries out of the way, we now move on to the biggest package, javax.net.ssl.

In discussing usage of the javax.net.ssl package, we will begin from the inside out. Note that all of these classes are either interfaces or abstract, so although the developer writes to these framework classes, there will have to also be an implementation that slides into this framework.

SSLSession

SSLSession will represent a security context that has completed negotiation between the two peers in an SSL connection. With an SSLSession firmly in hand, developers may inquire as to the SSL cipher suite that is currently being used between the two endpoints. The answer to this inquiry (getCipherSuite()) is a Java String, and for Sun's JSSE may take on the following values:

- SSL_RSA_WITH_RC4_128_MD5 – a non-exportable (North America-only) SSL version 3 cipher suite supporting 128-bit RC4 encryption keys and full RSA key sizes

- SSL_DHE_DSS_WITH_3DES_EDE_CBC_SHA – a non-exportable SSL version 3 cipher suite supporting 168-bit DES (Data Encryption Standard) encryption keys (however, the effective strength of the cipher is limited to 112 bits)

- SSL_DH_anon_EXPORT_WITH_DES40_CBC_SHA – an exportable SSL version 3 cipher suite using weakened DES encryption, and which doesn't actually support even server authentication

- SSL_RSA_WITH_NULL_MD5 – an exportable SSL version 3 cipher suite using no encryption, but full RSA key size

- SSL_CK_RC4_128_EXPORT40_WITH_MD5 – an exportable SSL version 2 cipher suite using weakened RC4 encryption and limited RSA key sizes.

Perhaps even more interesting is the ability to discover something about the entity on the other end of the connection. There are two methods that may be of use here, getPeerHost() and getPeerCertificateChain(). The getPeerHost() method returns the host name of the peer. For the server, the peer host name would be the client machine name, and for the client, it would be the server machine name. It should be noted however that these names were not authenticated, so they are of limited use in any security checks.

The getPeerCertificateChain()method returns the array of X.509 certificates that was presented by the peer. For the client, this method would thus return the server's certificate and chain, and for the server, this method would return the client's certificate (if SSL V3 and using client-side certificates). The certificates were validated as part of the SSL session establishment protocol (*handshake*), and can be trusted. Thus, these certificates are more profitably employed in security checks than the unauthenticated name of the partner machine.

There are a few other methods that deal with time of session establishment, etc., and these methods could be employed in an application that was trying to thoroughly manage SSL connections. We've talked about SSLSession objects, but how can a developer obtain one of these objects? The only way to get an SSLSession is to retrieve it from an SSLSocket with a getSession() call.

SSLSocket

SSLSocket extends java.net.Socket, adding methods appropriate to secure sessions. An SSLSocket, when first created, is an unprotected TCP socket. Until the process known as *handshaking* is complete, the data flows in the clear. To complete the handshake, the client and server sides of the SSL connection must agree upon what kind of encryption is going to be used, and make sure that they can accept each other's proof of identity. Developers have the opportunity to participate in part of the handshake setup, as they can influence what cipher suites can be used on the connection. Of course, they do not have complete power, as the underlying SSL implementation classes have to be able to carry out their wishes. The cipher suites must be available to both the client and server, for example. Another point to note is that if the developer does not want to know anything about the handshaking or cipher suites, they can just begin to transmit data over the SSLSocket, and all the handshaking will happen automatically to protect the data in transit.

Developers can ask the underlying implementation what cipher suites are supported by calling getSupportedCipherSuites(). Then the program can sift through the String array that is returned, eliminating ciphers that are not to the programmer's liking, and then call setEnabledCipherSuites() to pass in just the selections that they desire. This may not always succeed, however, as the other side of the SSL connection must agree to one of the ciphers selected (so usually developers allow the SSL implementation full freedom to select a cipher suite, which is simply done by not calling setEnabledCipherSuites() at all, which would allow the SSLSocket implementation to select from all possible supported suites). The application triggers the handshake by calling the startHandshake() method, or, as mentioned above, by just starting data transmission. The first time this is done on an SSLSocket, the call is synchronous and nothing further happens until the socket is secure, or the attempt to set up SSL with these particular parameters fails. Once secure communications have succeeded at least one time on an SSLSocket, subsequent calls to startHandshake() are asynchronous, and if developers care to know when the handshake has completed, they must actually register a listener via addHandshakeCompletedListener(), which will use the normal Java Beans event/listener interface to signal handshake completion.

SSLServerSocket

The server-side companion to SSLSocket is SSLServerSocket, which extends java.net.ServerSocket. It has fewer methods than SSLSocket, as it is missing all the methods associated with handshaking, implying that the client side of the connection is driving the handshaking. The most important method that it has that SSLSocket lacks is the accept() method, whereby the server side of a socket can wait for a connection attempt to be made.

Since both the SSLSocket and SSLServerSocket classes themselves are abstract, it is fair for developers to ask how they can get an instantiation of this class that they can operate on with these methods. Developers can get a reference to an implementation of SSLSocket from a number of different createSocket() calls on an SSLSocketFactory, or from an accept() call on an SSLServerSocket.

SSLSocketFactory

SSLSocketFactory extends javax.net.SocketFactory to create secure sockets. To be more precise, it provides a static getDefault() method that locates the underlying implementation class, either by examining the ssl.SocketFactory.provider property in the java.security file or by choosing the implementation class that Sun provides in their JSSE distribution. Note that developers need to have added the JSSE provider to the security provider list, or the administrator should have configured J2SE to know about the JSSE provider. Since the rest of SSLSocketFactory consists of abstract methods, the implementation class has the job to provide implementations of the methods that SSLSocketFactory describes, which can be summed up as a variety of Socket creation calls, including a few that deal directly with cryptography. One method that is of interest is a createSocket() method that takes as an input parameter an already extant java.net.Socket. This capability would permit interesting capabilities such as converting a socket to SSL after having tunneled on it.

SSLServerSocketFactory

The SSLServerSocketFactory class serves to create the server side of a secure connection (and extend javax.net.ServerSocketFactory). It works like the SSLSocketFactory, except that it looks for the ssl.ServerSocketFactory.provider property in the java.security file. Once a developer has a reference to an implementation of SSLServerSocketFactory, no doubt through SSLServerSocketFactory.getDefault(), the developer can create ServerSockets through a number of different createServerSocket calls.

Before moving on from the factory classes, it is worth discussing their utility. There are classes and methods that need to know that their transmissions are secure, but do not need to know which implementation was used. These classes and methods can make use of SSLSocketFactory or SSLServerSocketFactory. There are other classes and methods that may need communication in a way that satisfies their caller, but this might either be a normal, unprotected socket, which is much better for performance, or a secure socket. In the secure case, these classes and methods would have a signature that would take either a SocketFactory or a ServerSocketFactory and the caller would pass a reference to an SSLSocketFactory or an SSLServerSocketFactory when they needed secure communications. The sample programs later in this article illustrate such usage.

At this point, we have covered most of the important objects and methods in the JSSE framework. Unfortunately, the JSSE 1.0 API is not quite complete, and there is some functionality buried in the Sun provider that may be necessary to properly manage SSL, especially as the developer looks at the server side of the APIs. What we are referring to are the trust management and key management APIs.

To complete an SSL connection, both the client and server sides of the application must agree on a cipher suite. Typically, this means that the server must present a public key certificate signed by an authority that the client recognizes, which means that the client must have a certificate for that authority in its database of trusted authorities. Web browsers finesse this requirement by including a database of trusted authorities, so browser users may be fortunate enough to never have to deal with this issue.

The Java platform includes a default set of trusted authorities in a KeyStore in a default location with a default password. In the Java 2 SDK Version 1.2, this default KeyStore only recognizes VeriSign-signed or Thawte-signed server certificates. If developers and users are only using the client side of JSSE and their application is talking to a server that is using a server certificate obtained from VeriSign or Thawte, they can be blissfully unaware of these issues, and the JSSE specification seems complete. However, once developers and users take on the server side of JSSE, or if they are talking to a server that has a server certificate signed by a Certificate Authority (CA) other than VeriSign or Thawte, they must dip below the JSSE framework classes into provider-specific functionality to make this work. As before, the sample program will serve to illustrate this. Since this is really outside the JSSE framework, we will only cover the bare minimum for an understanding of the sample.

SSLContext

This class serves as a factory for secure socket factories. It has a constructor that allows the programmer to plug in a keystore other than the default, and both getSocketFactory() and getServerSocketFactory() methods. It also has a static getInstance() method whereby we can retrieve a provider for the secure protocol of choice, either SSL or Transport Layer Security (TLS).

TrustManagerFactory and KeyManagerFactory

These classes abstract the authentication mechanism and the actual cryptographic key material to use in authentication. In the sample program, we use X.509 public key certificates (the only choice in this version of JSSE).

java.security.KeyStore

This class, part of J2SE, provides a secure way to store certificates. In the sample program, we read certificates in through the normal JKS format. The Sun JSSE implementation allows reading (no support for writing, though) certificates from a PKCS12 format as well. To make this particular program function, we generate a self-signed certificate, build a Java KeyStore with this certificate and appropriate passwords, put the KeyStore on both the client and server sides, and let SSLContext know that it should use it.

Sample Programs

The sample programs are contained in five source files. There is a ClientMain and a ServerMain, and then a ClientPiece and a ServerPiece, as well as some statics in a file called MySSLConstants. The pieces are responsible for doing the actual I/O, and are oblivious as to whether the sockets that they are using are SSLSockets or not. Both the main routines locate SocketFactory objects and SSLSocket objects and construct pieces that allow them to do either encrypted I/O over SSLSocket objects or regular I/O over normal Socket objects. Both of the main routines also take care of the necessary key management details, given that the programs are using a self-signed certificate in a custom KeyStore file. The last two listings show the output from both the server and client windows.

ClientMain.java

```
package ibm.book;

import javax.net.SocketFactory;
import javax.net.ssl.SSLSocketFactory;
import java.net.Socket;
import java.net.SocketException;
import java.io.IOException;
// These imports are only necessary to accomodate KeyMgmt and TrustMgmt
import java.security.KeyStore;
import com.sun.net.ssl.SSLContext;
import com.sun.net.ssl.KeyManagerFactory;
import com.sun.net.ssl.TrustManagerFactory;
import com.sun.net.ssl.TrustManager;
import java.io.FileInputStream;
// End of imports only necessary to accomodate KeyMgmt and TrustMgmt

public class ClientMain {
    public static void main(String argv[]) {

        ClientPiece hidden, notHidden;
        boolean using_cacerts = false;
        SocketFactory sssf = null;

        // Add the JSSE provider to the list of security providers
        java.security.Security.insertProviderAt(
            new com.sun.net.ssl.internal.ssl.Provider(),1);

        // Find a SocketFactory for vanilla sockets
        SocketFactory mssf = SocketFactory.getDefault();

        try {
            notHidden = new ClientPiece(mssf, MySSLConstants.unprotectedPort);
        }
        catch (IOException ioe) {
            System.out.println(
                "Could not create a ClientPiece around an 'insecure' socket");
```

```
        ioe.printStackTrace();
        return;
    }

    // Find an SSLSocketFactory

    if (using_cacerts) {
        // If we could rely on cacerts, this would be sufficient
        sssf = SSLSocketFactory.getDefault();
    }
    else {
        try {
            // Not relying on cacerts, have our own keystore
            // Set up trust/key management
            KeyStore ks = KeyStore.getInstance("JKS");
            ks.load(new FileInputStream("testkeys"),
                "passphrase".toCharArray());
            KeyManagerFactory kmf = KeyManagerFactory.getInstance("SunX509");
            kmf.init(ks, "passphrase".toCharArray());
            TrustManagerFactory tmf =
                TrustManagerFactory.getInstance("SunX509");
            tmf.init(ks);
            SSLContext myContext = SSLContext.getInstance("SSL");
            myContext.init(kmf.getKeyManagers(), tmf.getTrustManagers(), null);
            sssf = myContext.getSocketFactory();
        }
        catch (Exception e) {
            System.out.println("Could not set up keystore");
            e.printStackTrace();
            System.exit(1);
        }
        System.out.println("Successfully set up keystore");
    }

    System.out.println("The 'secure' socket factory is "
        + sssf.getClass().getName());
    try {
        hidden = new ClientPiece(sssf, MySSLConstants.protectedPort);
    }
    catch (IOException ioe) {
        System.out.println("Could not create a secure socket");
        ioe.printStackTrace();
        return;
    }
```

```
    // OK, all set up
    // Let's see if anyone wants to listen

    for (int i=0; i<10; i++) {
        try {
            System.out.println("Writing to secure socket");
            hidden.talk("Writing to secure socket");
            System.out.println("Writing to insecure socket");
            notHidden.talk("Writing to insecure socket");
        }
        catch (SocketException se) {
            se.printStackTrace();
            break;
        }
        catch (IOException ioe) {
            ioe.printStackTrace();
            break;
        }
    }

    try {
        hidden.talk("Done");
        System.out.println("Response on secure socket is "+hidden.listen());
        notHidden.talk("Done");
        System.out.println("Response on insecure socket is "
            + notHidden.listen());
    }
    catch (IOException ioe) {
        ioe.printStackTrace();
    }
  }
}
```

ClientPiece.java

```
package ibm.book;

import java.io.DataInputStream;
import java.io.DataOutputStream;
import java.io.IOException;
import java.net.InetAddress;
```

```
import java.net.Socket;
import javax.net.SocketFactory;
/*
 * Provide an abstraction of Sockets that is SSL-oblivious
 * The caller passes in a Factory, and we just build 'em
 */

class ClientPiece {

    private Socket socket;
    DataOutputStream dos;
    DataInputStream dis;

    ClientPiece(SocketFactory socketFactory, int port)
        throws java.io.IOException {

        socket = socketFactory.createSocket(InetAddress.getLocalHost(), port);
        dos = new DataOutputStream(socket.getOutputStream());
        dis = new DataInputStream(socket.getInputStream());
    }

    void talk(String text) throws java.io.IOException {
        dos.writeUTF(text);
        dos.flush();
    }

    String listen() throws java.io.IOException {
        return dis.readUTF();
    }
}
```

ServerMain.java

```
package ibm.book;

import javax.net.ServerSocketFactory;
import javax.net.ssl.SSLServerSocketFactory;
import java.net.ServerSocket;
import java.net.SocketException;
import java.io.IOException;
// These imports are only necessary to accomodate KeyMgmt and TrustMgmt
import java.security.KeyStore;
```

```
import com.sun.net.ssl.SSLContext;
import com.sun.net.ssl.KeyManagerFactory;
import com.sun.net.ssl.TrustManagerFactory;
import com.sun.net.ssl.TrustManager;
import java.io.FileInputStream;
// End of imports only necessary to accomodate KeyMgmt and TrustMgmt

public class ServerMain {

    public static void main(String argv[]) {

        ServerPiece hidden = null, notHidden = null;
        boolean using_cacerts = false;
        ServerSocketFactory sssf = null;

        // Add the JSSE provider to the list of security providers
        java.security.Security.insertProviderAt(
            new com.sun.net.ssl.internal.ssl.Provider(),1);

        // Find a ServerSocketFactory for unprotected sockets
        ServerSocketFactory mssf = ServerSocketFactory.getDefault();
        try {
            notHidden = new ServerPiece(mssf, MySSLConstants.unprotectedPort);
        }
        catch (IOException ioe) {
            System.out.println(
                "Could not create a ServerPiece around an 'insecure' socket");
            ioe.printStackTrace();
            System.exit(1);
        }

        // Find an SSLServerSocketFactory for SSL sockets

        if (using_cacerts) {
            // If we could rely on cacerts, this would be sufficient
            sssf = SSLServerSocketFactory.getDefault();
        }
        else {
            try {
                // Not relying on cacerts, have our own keystore
                // Set up trust/key management
                KeyStore ks = KeyStore.getInstance("JKS");
                ks.load(new FileInputStream("testkeys"),
                    "passphrase".toCharArray());
```

```
        KeyManagerFactory kmf = KeyManagerFactory.getInstance("SunX509");
        kmf.init(ks, "passphrase".toCharArray());
        TrustManagerFactory tmf =
            TrustManagerFactory.getInstance("SunX509");
        tmf.init(ks);
        SSLContext myContext = SSLContext.getInstance("SSL");
        myContext.init(kmf.getKeyManagers(), tmf.getTrustManagers(), null);
        // Now have a Factory of Factories !
        sssf = myContext.getServerSocketFactory();
    }
    catch (Exception e) {
        e.printStackTrace();
        System.exit(1);
    }
    System.out.println("Successfully set up keystore");
}

System.out.println("SSLServerSocketFactory name is "
    + sssf.getClass().getName());
try {
    hidden = new ServerPiece(sssf, MySSLConstants.protectedPort);
}
catch (IOException ioe) {
    System.out.println("Could not create a secure socket");
    ioe.printStackTrace();
    System.exit(1);
}

// OK, all set up
// Let's see if anyone wants to talk

for (;;) {
    try {
        System.out.println("Reading from secure socket");
        hidden.echo();
        System.out.println("Reading from insecure socket");
        notHidden.echo();
    }
    catch (SocketException se) {
        se.printStackTrace();
        break;
    }
```

```
        catch (IOException ioe) {
            ioe.printStackTrace();
            break;
        }
    }
  }
}
```

ServerPiece.java

```
package ibm.book;

import java.io.DataInputStream;
import java.io.DataOutputStream;
import java.io.IOException;
import java.net.ServerSocket;
import java.net.Socket;
import javax.net.ServerSocketFactory;

/*
 * Provide an abstraction of ServerSockets that is SSL-oblivious
 * The caller passes in a Factory, and we just build 'em
 */

class ServerPiece {

    static Class sslServerSocketClass;
    private ServerSocket serverSocket;
    private Socket inbound = null;
    DataInputStream dis = null;
    DataOutputStream dos = null;

    ServerPiece(ServerSocketFactory serverSocketFactory, int port)
        throws java.io.IOException {

        System.out.println("ServerSocketFactory is "
            + serverSocketFactory.getClass().getName());
        serverSocket = serverSocketFactory.createServerSocket(port);
        if (serverSocket.getClass().isInstance(sslServerSocketClass)) {
            System.out.println("Creating an SSL Server Socket");
        }
        System.out.println("Server socket is "
```

```
                + serverSocket.getClass().getName());
    }
    void echo() throws java.io.IOException {
        if (inbound == null) {
            inbound = serverSocket.accept();
            System.out.println("Type of socket is "+inbound.getClass().getName());
            dis = new DataInputStream(inbound.getInputStream());
            dos = new DataOutputStream(inbound.getOutputStream());
        }
        System.out.println("Processing server request");
        String inputData = dis.readUTF();
        System.out.println("Data is \n\t"+inputData);
        if (inputData.equals("Done")) { // Send reply
            dos.writeUTF("Ok");
            dos.flush();
            inbound.close();
            inbound = null;
            dis = null;
            dos = null;
        }
    }

    static { // Get a reference to the SSLServerSocket class
        try {
            sslServerSocketClass = Class.forName("javax.net.ssl.SSLServerSocket");
        }
        catch (ClassNotFoundException cnfe) {
        }
    }
}
```

MySSLConstants.java

```
package ibm.book;

public interface MySSLConstants {
    public static final int unprotectedPort   =   6999;
    public static final int protectedPort      =   6998;
}
```

Output from server window

```
C:\>java ibm.book.ServerMain
ServerSocketFactory is javax.net.DefaultServerSocketFactory
Server socket is java.net.ServerSocket
Successfully set up keystore
SSLServerSocketFactory name is
com.sun.net.ssl.internal.ssl.SSLServerSocketFactoryImpl
ServerSocketFactory is com.sun.net.ssl.internal.ssl.SSLServerSocketFactoryImpl
Server socket is com.sun.net.ssl.internal.ssl.SSLServerSocketImpl
Reading from secure socket
Type of socket is com.sun.net.ssl.internal.ssl.SSLSocketImpl
Processing server request
Data is
        Writing to secure socket
Reading from insecure socket
Type of socket is java.net.Socket
Processing server request
Data is
        Writing to insecure socket
Reading from secure socket
Processing server request
...
Some lines deleted here
...
Reading from secure socket
Processing server request
Data is
        Done
Reading from insecure socket
Processing server request
Data is Done
Reading from secure socket
```

Output from client window

```
C:\>java ibm.book.ClientMain
Successfully set up keystore
The 'secure' socket factory is
com.sun.net.ssl.internal.ssl.SSLSocketFactoryImpl
Writing to secure socket
Writing to insecure socket
```

```
Writing to secure socket
Writing to insecure socket
Writing to secure socket
Writing to insecure socket
Writing to secure socket
Writing to insecure socket
Writing to secure socket
Writing to insecure socket
Writing to secure socket
Writing to insecure socket
Writing to secure socket
Writing to insecure socket
Writing to secure socket
Writing to insecure socket
Writing to secure socket
Writing to insecure socket
Writing to secure socket
Writing to insecure socket
Writing to secure socket
Writing to insecure socket
Response on secure socket is Ok
Response on insecure socket is Ok
```

Summary

JSSE is a very useful extension to the basic Java communication capabilities, providing data privacy, authentication and data integrity. The three JSSE packages provide a robust foundation for establishing secure connections between client and server applications. JSSE could be enhanced, but developers need not wait for nirvana – there's data out there that needs protecting!

Other Security Issues

In this last section, we introduce two important security technologies: JAAS and Kerberos. The Java Authentication and Authorization Services (JAAS) package has become an essential part of J2SE version 1.3. Kerberos is an older security technology, but it is still in mainstream use today. Finally, we give you specific hints and tips to writing robust and secure Java code.

- All that JAAS: An overview of the Java Authentication and Authorization Services

- A Kerberos primer

- Crafting robust and secure Java code

All that JAAS: An overview of the Java Authentication and Authorization Services

In 1999, Sun published the specification for a new standard extension. The acronym for the extension is JAAS (pronounced "jazz"), which stands for *Java Authentication and Authorization Services*. This article presents an overview of JAAS: What it is, why it was created, and some of the rationale behind the current design.

JAAS extends the Java 2 security model

The current Java 2 security model provides fine-grained, policy-based access control for both applets and applications. The permission model takes into account the physical origin (the directory or URL) of the classes that currently are active, as well as their logical origin, the identity of the organization that produced the classes, as proved by digital signature. This model serves well the browsers that first popularized the Java language, as it deals effectively with the issues of mobile code.

JAAS augments the current Java 2 runtime to add an awareness of the user trying to run the applet or application and augments the Java 2 security model to allow both the specification of permissions that take into account a user's identity and to enforce these permissions at runtime. The first augmentation is what would be referred to as *Authentication*. The latter two additions would be referred to as *Authorization*.

JAAS extends the reach of Java technologies

The Java platform already enjoys success on the desktop and in the browser. For Java technologies to capture the enterprise backend environment, it needs to interact with secure operating systems, resource managers and applications that today are concerned about the identity of the person or computer attempting to execute the code. JAAS allows Java programs to interact with underlying security applications, learn what the current identities are, possibly modulate these identities (for example, *log in*), reflect these identities to the Java runtime and enforce access controls specified in terms of these identities.

JAAS goals

JAAS is designed with several goals in mind:

1.   JAAS allows *simple*, pluggable authentication, which means that the authentication interfaces are designed to hide as much complexity as possible. *Pluggable authentication* means that the interfaces are abstract enough that alternate authentication mechanisms should be able to be substituted without security-casual applications needing to know or care.

2.   JAAS allows *policy-based authentication*, which means that security-casual applications need not concern themselves with the exact authentication mechanisms currently in use. The default login configuration mechanism for JAAS is a configuration file, so that applications need neither know nor care what authentication is happening.

3.   JAAS allows *stackable authentication*, which means that multiple authentication mechanisms might need to be successful before an authorized context is established. For example, to run the "testDB2" application, a Kerberos login and a DB2 login are required.

4.   JAAS allows user-based permissions to be a *simple extension* of the current permission model, which means that the current Java 2 permission model is preserved and that the additional capability is provided in an extensible, easily understood way.

Fundamental abstractions in JAAS

Now that the overview-level features and goals of JAAS have been covered, it's time to *open the hood* and examine JAAS in somewhat greater detail. JAAS is contained in several packages rooted at javax.security.auth, with some implementation classes in vendor-specific packages.

One of the first issues that the JAAS designers wrestled with was how to represent the *user, machine* or the *authenticated identity* with which we wish to associate permissions. Earlier versions of Java security moved in the direction of using java.security.Identity, which is a class (now deprecated) that said that users had a name and java.security.Certificates with which to prove identity. Identity's biggest drawback was its insistence that Certificates were an essential part of an authenticated identity. Since Certificates are obviously not part of all authentication mechanisms, JAAS designers rejected Identity on the grounds of insufficient generality. Another strong contender was java.security.Principal, which is a simple interface whose main method is simply a getName() method that returns a java.lang.String.

The JAAS designers opted to go with java.security. Principal, because it seemed that all authentication mechanisms (to be usable) represent users as having a printable name.

Having decided that Principal would be a key abstraction, the next issue was how to aggregate them to represent an authenticated context. Since one of the JAAS goals was to allow stackable authentication, it was obvious that one could easily end up with multiple Principals in one authenticated context. So, without much discussion, javax.security.auth.Subject was chosen to represent this collection of Principals.

With somewhat more controversy, the JAAS designers concluded that Principals may have some sort of proof of identity that they need to be able to provide at a moment's notice, and these proofs of identity may include sensitive information, so a set of public credentials and a set of private credentials were also added to Subject. Since the content of a credential may vary widely across authentication mechanisms, from a simple password to a fingerprint (to infinity and beyond!), the type of a credential was simply left as java.lang.Object. Relationships between Principals and credentials, if any, were left as an exercise for the implementer of the particular Principal class (or more likely, the particular LoginModule class). From a JAAS perspective, the only difference between private and public credentials is that a particular

javax.security.auth.AuthPermission is required for access to the set of private credentials.

Enabling a Java program for JAAS

An important feature in the JAAS design is the mechanism by which an authenticated context is set up. Given a multitude of situations in which authentication is unnecessary, the JAAS designers did not want to make it part of the normal dispatch path for a class or instance method. Thus it was decided that if a Java program wishes to request whatever authentication has been requested for it, it should construct a javax.security.auth.LoginContext and call its login() method. This annotates a Subject with appropriate authenticated identities. To assume the identity of that Subject, the program calls Subject.doAs(Subject,java.security.PrivilegedAction), which runs the specified PrivilegedAction as that Subject, then returns to the original security state. When the program has no further need of the authenticated identities, it can simply call the LoginContext logout() method. In keeping with the JAAS goal of simplicity, there are no parameters on either of these calls. There are parameters on the LoginContext constructor, however. The first of these is simply a java.lang.String. This is used as an index into a JAAS configuration file, which locates the appropriate LoginModule(s) to be used to authenticate the current user of the program.

The usage of this index is entirely up to the Java program, and could be a mechanism to deliberately select a particular type of authentication to be used. If the program is security-casual, it might simply pass in its own class name as the String and pick up whatever authentication had been configured for it. This would look something like:

```
LoginContext lc = new LoginContext(this.getClass().getName());
lc.login();
...
Subject.doAs(lc.getSubject(),somePrivilegedAction Instance);
...
lc.logout();
lc = null;
```

The additional constructors for LoginContext deal with some increasingly complex situations and are covered briefly with an example in the next section.

Dealing with all possible authentication mechanisms

Another of the issues that the JAAS designers had to wrestle with was the wide variety of authentication mechanisms and the various arguments that they might take. For example, authentication could be as simple as an account name (or user name) and a password or could require a distinguished name and the ability to prove identity through digital signature or could require a name and a fingerprint, or a retinal scan, or ad infinitum. Since one of the goals of JAAS was to have a pluggable authentication mechanism, the framework methods had to be generic enough to allow all authentication mechanisms to work and simple enough so that complexity need not be a hindrance to authentication mechanism providers. This issue is adroitly handled by having the four authentication methods visible at the javax.security.auth.spi.LoginModule API, login(), commit(), abort(), and logout() take absolutely no parameters, and return nothing (in programming, this is a return type of void). This approach certainly succeeds in not requiring authentication providers to add anything artificial to their current interfaces, but still leaves the issue of how to provide the additional information needed.

The mechanism for providing additional information is to have an initialize() method in each LoginModule, where one may or may not pass in a javax.security.auth.callback.CallbackHandler. These callback routines, if provided, can be used in an implementation- and environment-specific manner to gather additional information to satisfy the needs of the particular LoginModule. Translated, this means that if a LoginModule needs some information to authenticate the user, it can examine the array of Callbacks that it was initialized with to see if it has a mechanism to derive the necessary data. For example, if a userid and password are needed, the LoginModule can examine the Callback array to see if it contains a javax.security.auth.callback.NameCallback and a javax.security.auth.callback.PasswordCallback. If so, it can call them to attempt to get the necessary information.

Developers may wonder, "Just how did the Callback array get passed in to the initialize() method?" The answer is that one of the more complicated LoginContext constructors (that were glossed over earlier) takes a CallbackHandler and uses it when connecting to LoginModules.

Authorization

Now that the Authentication framework has been discussed, it is time to move on to a brief overview of the Authorization piece of JAAS. JAAS extends the Java 2 permission model to incorporate the idea of authenticated identities in the permission itself. This extension narrows the scope of the permission being granted to only the Principal specified in the permission. To illustrate, the following entry in a normal Java 2 policy file would grant READ access to the file "foo" to all classes in the codebase "http://gordo.austin.ibm.com/barnone":

```
grant codeBase http://gordo.austin.ibm.com/barnone/* {
    permission java.io.FilePermission "c:\\foo", "read";
};
```

In a JAAS-extended policy file, the following entry would grant READ access to the file "foo" to all classes in the codebase "http://gordo.austin.ibm.com/barsome," but only if the current Subject contained a principal (in this case, a com.ibm.security.auth.NTUserPrincipal) named "bob:"

```
grant codeBase http://gordo.austin.ibm.com/barsome/*,
    principal com.ibm.security.auth.NTUserPrincipal "bob"{
    permission java.io.FilePermission "c:\\foo", "read";
};
```

Additional information

There are a few other points that need to be made regarding JAAS. First, JAAS is intended to be the underpinning for the Java 2 Extended Edition (J2EE) Enterprise JavaBeans (EJB) security model. Given the importance of EJB in e-business, one may expect to see rapid adoption of JAAS. Additionally, JAAS is expected to be used as the underpinning for Remote Method Invocation (RMI) security enhancements.

Conclusion

The Java 2 platform security framework is an impressive base for secure computing in e-business. JAAS builds on this foundation to integrate more closely with secure operating systems, resource managers and applications on enterprise servers.

A Kerberos primer

If you have anything at all to do with computing, *Kerberos* is a term you may hear a lot about in the next few months. One of the reasons for this may be the public release of operating systems such as Windows 2000 or Solaris 8, which "incorporate Kerberos technology." Another reason may be stories about major Wall Street firms or national labs that incorporate Kerberos technology and have used Distributed Computing Environment (DCE)-based applications for years. Yet another reason may be the work that is happening in standards bodies to standardize Java interfaces for using Kerberos services. This article explains what Kerberos is and discusses some of its features.

Origins

Kerberos is a security protocol that originated at the Massachusetts Institute of Technology (MIT) as part of Project Athena in the 1980s. The research work that gave birth to Kerberos was a research paper by Needham and Schroeder that was published in 1978 (see references). This particular paper discussed using encryption for authentication over computer networks. Authentication is simply proving your identity. Encryption is simply scrambling data in such a way that only the appropriate recipient can reconstitute it.

So what is a *Kerberos*? Kerberos was the mythological three-headed dog that guarded the entrance to the underworld. Unless you could get past Kerberos, you could not enter (or leave!) the underworld. In much the same way, Kerberos guards the entrance to services on the networks.

Important features

Mutual authentication

Kerberos is an authentication protocol that identifies principals (users and services) by requiring them to present proof of identity. A very useful facet of Kerberos is that it provides for mutual authentication: not only do users of a service identify themselves to the service, but also users can challenge the service to prove its identity. In a world of very open networks like the Internet, this is a very comforting feature.

To accomplish the feat of mutual authentication, Kerberos makes use of what's called *trusted third-party authentication*. This means that the Kerberos server must know who all the parties are and how they prove their identity (their passwords). This concentration of secret information makes the Kerberos server (more technically known as the Key Distribution Center or KDC) a very important resource to protect and monitor. Of course, it also attracts the hackers because of its importance. (Recall the words of the notorious bank robber, who when asked why on earth he robbed banks, replied sagely, "Because that's where the money is.") More importantly, the physical security of the KDC must be guaranteed, as the actual computer(s) housing the KDC may be more vulnerable than the network protocols that shield the KDC.

The Kerberos protocol assumes that all network traffic is vulnerable to capture, examination and substitution. It also assumes that it needs to work correctly even in the face of these challenging assumptions. These environmental assumptions match quite well with today's open networks and keep Kerberos in the game despite its relative (for the Internet) antiquity.

So in an environment where all network traffic might be captured, how does one authenticate (or *log in*) to Kerberos? One cannot simply wrap the password up and send it over to the server (which is what happens with network protocols such as HTTP 1.0 and basic authentication). Anyone snooping packets off the network would know your password. So how does Kerberos fix this problem?

At a very simple level, Kerberos uses encryption technology. The user's password is utilized (while still on the user's workstation) to generate an encryption key. The key encrypts certain pieces of information that are exchanged with the KDC. After a few exchanges, the KDC returns information to the user that is usable only by software on the workstation that knows the temporary encryption key derived from the password. Now when users wish to contact a Kerberos-protected service, they first contact the Kerberos ticket-granting service and ask for a ticket to the service. A ticket is a chunk of information that proves the user's identity to the service; but it's encrypted in the services' long-term key so it's unintelligible to the user.

Without getting terribly bogged down in the details of which key is used when, Kerberos is going to return information to users and services that is useful to them if they can decrypt it. Users are able to decrypt the data if they are who they told Kerberos they were. Furthermore, Kerberos can make use of temporary keys wherever possible, to make it harder for hackers to break in. When a user and a service are interacting, they are doing so with a key that was specially generated just for this particular interaction and that expires within a relatively short period of time. The key lifetime is configurable, but it is usually good for hours, not days.

Data integrity

Assuming that packets may have been tampered with on their way either from the client to the service or from the service to the client, does it do any good at all to have authentication? Is there anything that can be done to prove not only who or what is on the other end of the wire, but also that the data is authentic? This authenticity is more commonly referred to as data integrity, and Kerberos once more applies encryption technology to offer this service. Assuming that the client and service have authenticated as above and now each knows the key for the current interaction (or session), we have all the pieces necessary to guarantee either data integrity or data confidentiality.

Since encryption is a costly operation in terms of time and CPU power, and we are only looking to ensure that the data is authentic; we need not encrypt all the data that is transmitted. Instead, an encrypted one-way hash is computed and transmitted with the plaintext data. Well, that is what happens, and Kerberos provides services to do it, but let's go through that statement a little more slowly and explain the terms used.

A *one-way hash* is a cryptographic operation that quickly transforms any arbitrary message into a very short sequence of bytes. *Quickly* here means hundreds of times faster than encryption. A good hashing algorithm is very sensitive to the contents of the original message such that even a small change in the message should yield a very different hash value. *one-way* means that one cannot reverse-engineer the hash to learn anything about the original contents of the message.

Kerberos encrypts the much-shorter one-way hash, and bundles that together with the "plaintext" data, which is the original, unmodified message. The sender can then transmit this package to the receiver, who can look at the package, see what algorithm was used for the one-way hash and quickly compute the hash. Then the receiver can decrypt the received encrypted one-way hash and compare it with the hash that was just computed. If the two hashes match, the receiver knows exactly who sent the message and knows that the message was transmitted without modification.

Data confidentiality

There are always occasions when it is insufficient merely to know with whom you're talking and that no one can successfully change the conversation without being detected. Sometimes, you need to know that the conversation is completely private. A more technical term for privacy is *data confidentiality* and once again Kerberos addresses this need. Kerberos provides services that encrypt the entire plaintext message and (optionally) computes a one-way hash of the ciphertext (the output from the encryption engine). The sender transmits the package to the receiver, who decrypts the ciphertext and (optionally) verify the authenticity of the data. Although the data integrity feature is optional, if one is using data confidentiality, it is usually done as the cost of computing, and encrypting the one-way hash is minor compared to the cost of encrypting the whole message.

Encryption is a costly operation, both in terms of processing power and time. If it were not, then data confidentiality would always be used. But it is, so it is important to allow applications to pick the level of protection that they need at the point where it is needed, and Kerberos provides this.

Vulnerabilities

We have described only the high-level mechanics of Kerberos. One may wonder how hackers might attack a Kerberos-secured network and what some of its vulnerabilities might be. One of the main vulnerabilities (outside of physical attacks on the machine housing the KDC) is the human element. The only entrance into the Kerberos protocol is where a user specifies a password to start the process. Users are apt to use a short, easy-to-remember password, like a word one might find in a dictionary. A hacker might capture packets from the initial authentication flows, generate encryption keys based on words found in dictionaries, encrypt some packets containing the fairly-predictable initial Kerberos data exchanges, and look for a match. Once a match is found, a hacker has the password to another user's Kerberos account, and they can access the network and do whatever that user could do.

A counter for this particular attack is not to allow common words to be used as passwords. The end-user impact is that it makes it harder to remember a password. Another counter is to use Public-Key Cryptography or smartcards for the initial authentication, which takes simple passwords completely out of the picture.

Summary

Kerberos has been incorporated into many different product offerings for several reasons. First, it was designed for an environment that closely resembles today's Internet. Second, it has withstood the test of time very well. Another pragmatic point is that the specification for Kerberos only deals with the network protocols; i.e., what the control flows might be and the format of the packets over the network. There are no published standards for application programming interfaces (APIs). This lack of API specification makes it relatively easy to incorporate Kerberos into a product and claim Kerberos compliance, since all that has to be done is obey the network protocol.

Although base Kerberos, itself, is still undergoing some changes, the direction that the industry seems to be taking is to offer up the services that Kerberos supplies, but to generalize the interfaces a bit so that they are not so Kerberos-specific and to standardize on these more generic APIs. This approach is an acknowledgement of the great work that was originally done in the design of Kerberos. Even 15-20 years later not much is being added to base Kerberos except to generalize and then standardize services akin to those originally envisioned by Kerberos' creators. These efforts to create a more generic security API are known as *Generic Security Service Application Program Interface* or GSSAPI. There are even proposed standards for implementations of GSSAPI in the Java language that are close to acceptance, such as RFC 2853 (see http://www/ietf.org/rfc/rfc2853.txt), which would make Kerberos services that much more accessible to modern programming environments like the Java platform.

Crafting robust and secure Java code

To enthusiastic object-oriented programmers, it is the Java language that is important. It contains a number of important differences from C++, which reduce the chance of writing a rogue program by accident, as well as making it more difficult to write a rogue program by design. This article is intended to help you write code without compromising security.

Privileged Code Guidelines

A new feature implemented for the first time in Java 2 security is the lexical scoping of privilege modification, which is a technique that enforces the least privileged mode. Using this technique, it is possible to enable only the execution of the piece of code that needs the privilege. All the sensitive code could therefore be added at one place and defined as privileged by calling the doPrivileged() method. (The doPrivileged() method belongs to the java.security.AccessController class.) Through the use of this method, Java 2 security provides a facility to mark Java code as being privileged and temporarily grant its callers some permissions that they normally would not enjoy by themselves.

As an example, assume application code has RuntimePermission to load a certain native library. It calls upon the loadLibrary service, which in order to accomplish its task, needs read access to the native library file. However, the client code does not have the appropriate FilePermission that allows it access to this file, and so if the entire execution thread were checked for the granted FilePermission, the operation would fail where it should have succeeded.

To solve this problem, the API for privileged blocks was designed to allow marking a code block as privileged. When a code block is marked as privileged, it can call services based on *its* permissions even if some of its callers do not have these permissions.

Use privileged code sparingly, if at all. First, write your code without using privileged blocks. If your code bumps into a security exception, then consider if you need to use privileged blocks.

Remember that when a privileged block gets executed within your code, it can access any resource your code has permissions to access, even if its callers do not have these permissions. For example, if your code is an installed standard extension (which by definition resides at the <java-home>/lib/ext directory), then by default (if the default policy file is not modified) it can load libraries, read any file, read system properties, etc. If these operations happen in privileged blocks, they can be completed on behalf of unprivileged clients. By enabling privileges for as short a period or scope as possible it is much easier to audit the code to make sure that it is only accessing the minimal number of protected resources.

One of the biggest pitfalls to watch out for is public methods and/or non-public methods that can get invoked by public methods that wrap privileged blocks that deal with *dirty* variables. Here *dirty* means the variables are set by the caller (i.e., passed in as parameters), and thus are not under the control of the privileged code.

Java Coding Rules

Security Manager

Before adding anything to java.lang.SecurityManager, sun.Applet.AppletSecurity, or your own SecurityManager, run your changes by your local security group as changes can adversely affect the security of your Java environment.

Mutability

In general, be careful with any mutable static states that can cause unintended interactions between supposedly independent subsystems. Make your object immutable if possible. If you can't, make them cloneable and return copies. If you return things like arrays, Vectors, Hashtables, etc., remember that these objects are not immutable, and the caller can change the contents of these objects, which may have security implications. Additionally, immutable objects can improve concurrency, since no locking is needed. Consider the following immutability rules:

- Do not add any non-final public static variables to new code. For existing code, all non-final public static variables should be carefully reviewed.

- Do not create static states that can be modified via accessor methods, which do not perform any access permission checks.

- Never return a reference to an internal array containing sensitive data. For example, if your array contains objects that are immutable (such as Strings), you need to return a copy, otherwise the caller can change which Strings are in the array. Instead of passing back an array, make a copy of the array and pass that array.

- Never store a user specified array of objects directly. Constructors and methods taking arrays of objects, such as arrays of PublicKeys, should clone the arrays before saving them internally rather then directly assigning the array reference to an internal variable of similar type. Otherwise, any changes made by the user to the external array (after creating the object using the constructor in question) could accidentally change the internal state of the object though the object might otherwise be immutable.

There may be cases where it is desirable to reduce the dependency on a global state, but where eliminating the use of the global state entirely is not required, since the removal effort could be a significant amount of work and could create a large set of compatibility problems as well.

- A *final* class field or instance field holding a primitive value (int, short, long, float, double, byte, char, boolean, object reference) is a constant. (The primitives values (e.g., 5.05, *true*, 443, 'c') are immutable.) A primitive field not declared *final* is mutable.

```
final int one = 1;          // "one" is immutable
float pi = 3.14159          // "pi" is mutable since it is not final
// The reference to the Foo object below is immutable.
// However, the content of the Foo instance may be mutable.
final Foo obj = new Foo();
```

- A field declared *static* is a class field, which means that there is only one copy of the field once the class is initialized. This is comparable to a global variable.

```
class foo {
static final int constantOne = 1;    // a class constant
final int constantTwo = 2;      // an instance constant (non-static)
. . .
}
```

- Arrays contents are *always* mutable, even if the primitives it contains or objects it references are immutable. An array reference may be declared *final*, but only the reference to the array is immutable, but not the array's contents.

```
class bar {
// The reference to the array (dimensions) is immutable,
// but the individual elements can be changed.
static final int dimensions[] = { 500, 400 }; // mutable array contents
. . .
}
```

In general, an object (an instance of a class) is considered mutable if instances or the class contains any mutable fields, objects or arrays. In the previous example, class bar is a mutable class since the dimensions class field contains a mutable array.

Protected methods/fields

Review all the protected methods and/or fields, as they could be sensitive. In particular make sure that any method that copies a shared StringBuffer field is private and not protected.

Package-private methods/fields

Review all the *package* private methods and/or fields to see which could be made private. Where possible, make methods and fields private instead of package-private to avoid package-insertion attacks.

Public methods/fields

Use caution when declaring public variables; let your interface be through accessor methods. This way, it is possible to add centralized access control checks, if required.

Make sure that any public method that has access to and/or modifies internal state that is sensitive includes an access control check. In the following example it is possible that an untrusted code can set the value for TimeZone.

```
private static TimeZone  defaultZone = null;
public static synchronized void setDefault(TimeZone zone) {
    defaultZone = zone;
}
```

Exceptions

In general, do not catch a system-generated AccessControlException or SecurityException. Allow the security exception to propagate to the caller. If you must catch the exception to free a resource, for example, rethrow the original exception and instead of a new exception. The first exception will include the full callstack that generated the original error.

Native methods

Native code is inherently dangerous as it operates outside the security protections that the Java platform automatically provides. Avoid using native code where possible. When you must use native code, ensure that it does not bypass any security checks that you need to perform, and be alert that native code can change the contents of objects passed to it. Also, avoid method calls that bypass package boundaries, thus bypassing package protection.

Finalizer attacks

You may sometimes want to allow only trusted code to create instances of a class, so as to prohibit untrusted code from calling protected methods of this class. Say you write Class A. To prohibit untrusted code from creating instances of Class A, you may add security checks in the class constructor. This may not be sufficient. The reason security checks in the constructor are not sufficient is that if someone may extend your class, they may still call protected methods of the class from the finalizer.

You can help prevent finalizer attacks by making your class final or by ensuring that your sensitive fields and methods are private, and not protected.

Clear Sensitive Information

When storing sensitive information, such as private keys, always keep it in mutable data types (such as arrays) rather than in immutable objects (such as Strings), so that this information can be explicitly cleared immediately after usage. For example, your code could fill a byte array containing the definition of a private key with zeros after the private key is no longer needed. The automatic garbage collection provided by the Java architecture will not always perform this task as the collector may never reclaim the used memory, or it may be reclaimed much later on.

Conclusion

This article covers the basic programming techniques to promote safe Java programming practices. With these techniques in hand, developers have the knowledge to review their existing code for potential security flaws and be able to write new code without introducing security flaws.

Conclusion

Security remains an essential component to any successful e-business application, especially to those in the Java and Internet realm. The Java platform will continue to evolve to include more and more security features in its core. To date, Java technologies have had the right content at the right time to accelerate their integration into key parts of the technological infrastructure. The use of Java technologies on the enterprise backend of e-business will continue to drive more and more security content into the Java platform, as witnessed by the growth of Java Specification Requests (JSRs) for additional security content. Security will always play a key role to the success of e-business, protecting sensitive information from those with nefarious intent.

Viva Internet security! Viva Java security!

IBM DeveloperToolbox

Get the e-business tools and information you need all year long.

The IBM DeveloperToolbox brings you the tools and information that you need to develop open, end-to-end e-business solutions that integrate legacy systems and capitalize on the new and growing opportunities available through the Internet. You can enrich your e-business applications, move your solutions to new platforms, help lower your cost of doing business and deliver your products to market faster with a subscription to the DeveloperToolbox.

171

Depending on your level of participation, your subscription to the DeveloperToolbox provides:

- Fast, convenient, one-source access to more than 1,000 leading-edge development tools to help you build solutions on 16 platforms;

- Web access to tools, white papers, technical tips with the very latest insights and information from IBM;

- CD sets giving you the flexibility to access the DeveloperToolbox information in the way that's right for you; and

- A technical magazine, a quarterly collection of printed technical articles, news briefs and "heads up" previews of the latest technology and strategies from IBM.

We'll also keep you updated on hot new technologies and platforms like XML, Java, DB2, WebSphere, Linux, and Windows 2000 by refreshing our online Web catalog frequently.

DeveloperToolbox is a key component of PartnerWorld for Developers. Commercial members of PartnerWorld for Developers can view or download content at the Professional Level using their member ID and password. Commercial members also can receive the DeveloperToolbox CDs for just the cost of manufacturing, shipping and handling.

Leveraging IBM technology can give you a competitive edge. A subscription to the DeveloperToolbox helps ensure you have the latest IBM technology at your fingertips all year long.

Choose the membership level that works for you...

You can tailor your participation in the DeveloperToolbox to match your development interests and requirements. Your subscription entitles you to unlimited Web access for all content in your subscription level. A set of CDs is available for customers who subscribe at the Professional and Enterprise levels.

Guest Level is available on the Web to any registered application developer. From our Web site at http://www.developer.ibm.com/devcon/, you can register, review and download sample source code, technical documents, hints and tips, utilities and Java and Internet tools. All at no cost to you.

Professional Level includes the content available in the Guest Level and adds the convenience of periodic CD updates and a subscription to the technical magazine. At this level you'll have access to more

IBM and non-IBM tools along with compilers, toolkits for IBM operating systems and IBM e-business servers giving you the tools to develop e-business server or operating system applications.

Enterprise Level builds on the Professional Level by adding a comprehensive test environment for the IBM Application Server Software for e-business. The e-business software servers include IBM WebSphere, DB2, MQSeries, IBM SecureWay and much more! The license agreement allows up to 10 copies of the contents to be used for developing and testing your solutions in a team environment. DeveloperToolbox Enterprise Level provides over 1000 tools and documents, making this the most comprehensive resource available for e-business developers using IBM technology.

Subscribe Today:

```
US              1-800-633-8266
Brazil          0800-111 426 r. 7498
Canada          1-800-561-5293
Argentina       0-800-44-426 92 Interno 2987
Australia       +61 2-9354 7684
Venezuela       800-1-5000
Europe          +45 48 101509
Japan           81-3-3249-7048
Mexico          5 270 5990 (D.F.)
Colombia        9800-17555 (Nacional)
Austria         0660 8705
Germany         0 130 828041
```

About the Authors

Theodore J. Shrader is an author and feature lead on the IBM Java Security project. He has written numerous patents and articles dealing with Internet and Java development, Web design, distributed computing, object-oriented design, and database architectures. He also is a co-author of an operating systems programming guide published by John Wiley and Sons. You can contact him at tshrader@us.ibm.com.

Bruce A. Rich is the team lead of the IBM Java Security project. He has been involved in software for 21 years, first in operating systems development, then in secure distributed file systems, and more recently in secure Web server applications and Java programming. He has filed a number of patents and contributed to a book on distributed computing. You can contact him at rbruce@us.ibm.com.

Anthony J. Nadalin's current assignment is Lead Architect for IBM Java Security. As senior architect for Java Security, he has responsibility for infrastructure design and development across IBM. He serves as the primary security liaison to JavaSoft for security design and development collaboration. You can contact him at drsecure@us.ibm.com.

References

Books

Gong, Li. *Inside Java 2 Platform Security*. 1999. Addison Wesley, Reading, Massachusetts.

Knudsen, Jonathan. *Java Cryptography*. 1998. O'Reilly & Associates, Sebastopol, California.

Oaks, Scott. *Java Security*. 1998. O'Reilly & Associates, Sebastopol, California.

Pistoia, Marco, et al. *Java 2 Network Security*. 1999. International Business Machines Corporation, Research Triangle Park, North Carolina.

Tung, Brian. *Kerberos, A Network Authentication System*. 1999. Addison Wesley, Reading, Massachusetts.

Web Sites

IBM developerWorks web site: http://www.ibm.com/developer/.

IBM DeveloperToolbox web site: http://www.developer.ibm.com/devcon/.

IBM WebSphere preview technologies for Windows:
http://www7b.boulder.ibm.com/wsdd/wspvtindex.html

JavaSoft Java Security web site: http://java.sun.com/security/.

RSA PKCS web site: http://www.rsasecurity.com/rsalabs/pkcs/.

RSA S/MIME web site: http://www.rsasecurity.com/standards/smime/.

S/MIME working group: http://www.imc.org/ietf-smime/.

Index

A

C

D

E

G

H

I

K

J

K

U

URL, xvi, 7, 10, 13, 15-17, 20, 23, 25, 79, 100, 105, 129-132, 152

V

Verify, 42, 61, 67, 73-74, 76-80, 82, 84, 86, 88-93, 95, 97-98, 103, 105-107, 112-114, 117, 160

W

Web browser, 23-27, 77-78, 112-113, 123-125

Web server, 23, 25-27, 125, 127, 175

Printed in Great Britain by
Amazon.co.uk, Ltd.,
Marston Gate.